formatio
TRADITION. EXPERIENCE.
TRANSFORMATION.

Formatio books from InterVarsity Press follow the rich tradition of the church in the journey of spiritual formation. These books are not merely about being informed, but about being transformed by Christ and conformed to his image. Formatio stands in InterVarsity Press's evangelical publishing tradition by integrating God's Word with spiritual practice and by prompting readers to move from inward change to outward witness. InterVarsity Press uses the chambered nautilus for Formatio, a symbol of spiritual formation because of its continual spiral journey outward as it moves from its center. We believe that each of us is made with a deep desire to be in God's presence. Formatio books help us to fulfill our deepest desires and to become our true selves in light of God's grace.

Seasons of the Soul

Stages of Spiritual Development

BRUCE DEMAREST

IVP Books

An imprint of InterVarsity Press
Downers Grove, Illinois

InterVarsity Press
P.O. Box 1400, Downers Grove, IL 60515-1426
World Wide Web: www.ivpress.com
E-mail: email@ivpress.com

InterVarsity Press® is the book-publishing division of InterVarsity Christian Fellowship/USA®, a
movement of students and faculty active on campus at hundreds of universities, colleges and schools
of nursing in the United States of America, and a member movement of the International Fellowship
of Evangelical Students. For information about local and regional activities, write Public Relations
Dept., InterVarsity Christian Fellowship/USA, 6400 Schroeder Rd., P.O. Box 7895, Madison, WI
53707-7895, or visit the IVCF website at <www.intervarsity.org>.

Design: Cindy Kiple
Images: Leonard Gertz/Getty Images

ISBN 978-0-8308-3535-5

Printed in the United States of America ∞

Library of Congress Cataloging-in-Publication Data

Demarest, Bruce A.
  Seasons of the soul: stages of spiritual development/Bruce
  Demarest
    p. cm.
  "Formatio."
  Includes bibliographical references and index.
  ISBN 978-0-8308-3535-5 (pbk.: alk. paper)
  1. Spiritual formation. 2. Faith development. 3. Christian life.
  1. Title.
  BV4509.5.D45 2009
  248.4—dc22

                                2009011828

P   22 21 20 19 18 17 16 15 14 13 12 11 10 9 8 7 6

Y   27 26 25 24 23 22 21 20 19

Contents

Acknowledgments

Above all, I thank Elsie, my lifelong partner and fellow pilgrim, for her patience and kindness extended to allow completion of this work. I am also grateful to students in Denver Seminary's Certificate and Master of Arts programs in Christian Formation and Soul Care, who through class interactions and personal conversations have greatly stimulated my thought. Appreciation also is due to Rev. Janet Buntrock for her skillful research on source notes.

Preface

"The Lord your God . . . went ahead of you

on your journey, in fire by night and in

a cloud by day, to search out places for you to

camp and to show you the way you should go."

DEUTERONOMY 1:32-33

CHRISTIAN LIFE: A JOURNEY

We enjoy journeying to pleasant places—to a magnificent national park, a peaceful seashore or a romantic overseas destination. We delight in the planning, the travel, the arrival and the stay itself, which together form the fabric of our exciting journey. Travel to interesting places renews and refreshes body and soul.

The journey is a prominent biblical metaphor for the Christian life from its beginning to its fulfillment. The Christian life is not an aimless wandering but a challenging and sometimes perplexing pilgrimage to spiritual maturity and ultimately to our heavenly home. As Larry Crabb points out, "Life is a journey toward a land we have not yet seen along a path we sometimes cannot find. It is a journey of the soul toward its destiny and its home." John Bunyan's classic work *Pilgrim's Progress* brilliantly described the journey's challenging course and its destination in the Celestial City.

Portraits of the journey loom large on the pages of Scripture. God called Abraham to pull up stakes and journey in faith from Ur of the Chaldeans to an unknown land (Gen 12:1-2). Launching the greatest journey in history, the Israelites under Moses fled slavery in Egypt, passed through the Red Sea, wandered forty years in the wilderness and crossed into the Promised Land. Luke tells the story of an elder son who journeyed to a far country where he engaged in extravagant living, only to come to his senses and journey back home. The Gospels depict Jesus journeying from Galilee through Palestine and then to Jerusalem to be crucified and resurrected. The movement Jesus launched came to be known as "the way" (Acts 18:25), with our Lord himself the pioneer (Heb 12:2) and the way (Jn 14:6) through this world. The letter to the Hebrews portrays the Christian life as a wandering pilgrimage through this fleeting world to the heavenly city (Heb 11:8-10, 13-16; 13:14).

The Christian life can be seen as a journey that is both individual and corporate. Each of us enters the world on our own and along the way confronts God in the solitude of our own heart. At the journey's end we will each stand before God at the judgment to give account of our lives. At the same time we travel in company with faithful brothers and sisters in Christ, who encourage us in our struggles and keep us pointed toward the goal. The homeward journey is both empowered by God and lived out by us. God graciously calls us on the journey, but we must respond to his offer with trust and obedience.

PATTERN OF THE JOURNEY
As a young person I was taught that becoming a Christian meant

that I had arrived. But trusting Christ as Savior is only the beginning of a lifelong process of spiritual transformation and training in discipleship. We begin the journey as spiritual infants, but God intends that we advance to spiritual adulthood. Paul wrote, "When I was a child, I talked like a child, I thought like a child, I reasoned like a child. When I became a man, I put the ways of childhood behind me" (1 Cor 13:11).

Our spiritual journeys occur in seasons or phases (some use the term *stages*), which Moses acknowledged concerning Israel's journey through the wilderness (Num 33:1-2). The church father Irenaeus underscored this truth. "The Creator is always the same, but those who are created must pass from a beginning and through a middle course, a growth, and progression. And it is for this progress and increase that God has formed them according to the word of Scripture, 'Increase and multiply.' " Pastoral theologian James Loder observed that "stage transition dynamics are a powerful and pervasive force throughout life."

Just as we develop physically and emotionally from childhood to adolescence, young adulthood, middle age, maturity and old age, Christians grow continuously as they move through the spiritual seasons. However, we also experience cycles in which we move back through earlier spiritual seasons. We revisit past fears and failures, and hopefully relearn important spiritual lessons as we do.

Rarely does spiritual growth advance in a straight line toward heaven; it's more like an upward spiral. The Christian spiritual journey involves starting and stopping, digressions, and sometimes even reversions to previous stages. While God invites us to grow and mature, we retain the freedom to resist his gracious call, and at times we may backtrack. Since pilgrim believers still retain the sinful nature in this life, our journeys of transformation are ongoing throughout our lives.

ANALOGIES FROM THE DEVELOPMENTAL SCIENCES

The human sciences have proposed some helpful insights into the process of growth and maturation. Developmental psychologists study human personality formation through various stages of the life cycle, paying close attention to environment. Since people are a complex unity of body and soul/spirit, the development of our minds and souls are interrelated. Both spirituality and traditional psychology concern themselves with the soul in its journey toward authenticity and maturity.

Research into the human life cycle supports the idea that we pass through spiritual seasons or phases. Psychologist Erik H. Erikson identified eight stages of psychosocial development. His research brought about greater appreciation for the developmental stages and critical transitions of the human life cycle. And Harvard psychologist Lawrence Kohlberg identified six sequential stages in the development of human moral reasoning. Erikson and Kohlberg influenced the thought of psychologist and Methodist minister James Fowler, who focuses specifically on the development of faith. Fowler's six-stage paradigm addresses the process of *how* a person comes to believe rather than *what* he or she believes. Fowler observes that the stages of faith development unfold in a spiral sequence where each stage builds on previous ones to form new capacities for faith. Erikson's, Kohlberg's and Fowler's work all support a view of human development in multiple phases, which I'll apply to the Christian life by looking at a journey model for the development of the soul.

A HELPFUL PARADIGM

Christian authorities have produced many paradigms or representations of the spiritual journey (see the appendix for several important examples). I find helpful, among others, the broad paradigm set forth by Old Testament scholar Walter Brueggemann, who proposes that the life of faith involves moving with God through a repetitive, threefold pattern.

The first phase of Brueggemann's model—spiritual beginnings—involves being securely *orientated* (located): that is, coming to faith, experiencing God's blessing and launching the spiritual journey. We can compare this stage to Israel's deliverance from Egypt. The second movement—spiritual trials—involves being painfully *disorientated* (dislocated): that is, experiencing struggles, doubts, crises and perhaps a dark night of the soul. This stage is like Israel's wilderness wandering. The third element of Brueggemann's pattern involves being securely *reorientated* (relocated): that is, experiencing spiritual renewal, a deepened relationship with God and joy supplanting despair. Israel's entry into Canaan is an example of this final stage.

According to Brueggemann, we can understand the Psalms—the prayer book that sustained Israel on its journey from Egypt to Canaan—as fitting under these three headings. Catholic scholar Richard Byrne agrees that "secure orientation, painful disorientation, and surprising reorientation are three foundational moments repeated throughout life's journey."

BIBLICAL AND HISTORICAL SOURCES

As we explore the contours of the spiritual journey, our primary source of information will be the Scriptures, the inspired Word of God. Here and there we will trace the journeys of leading biblical people in their struggles to know, love and serve God. We will also be guided by important writings from our Christian spiritual tradition. We in the church are heirs of a two-thousand-year treasury of Christian devotion that we sometimes fail to appreciate. The insights offered by godly authorities from the past represent graced commentaries on the spiritual life that can offer fresh perspectives for living the Christian life today. Furthermore, I will illustrate insights for the journey from the experiences of contemporary pilgrims on their challenging journeys (with names altered).

THE BOOK AND SPIRITUAL FORMATION

As we explore the dynamics and seasons of the spiritual journey, I hope you'll come to appreciate the full transformation we are called to. I trust that this study will offer broad guidelines for how present-day pilgrims can grow in spiritual and emotional maturity. Hopefully the book will enable us all to respond more authentically to God's holy initiatives in our lives and to become more effective disciples of Jesus, living and serving in a needy world. May this study help us manage seasons of testing and crisis, enrich our prayer experience, heal emotional and spiritual wounds, and deepen our relationship with Christ. May it also shed valuable light on how Christians attend to God's call, experience ongoing conversion, advance in holiness and serve God more effectively.

Understanding the seasons and dynamics of the spiritual journey will equip us to guide others more skillfully on their challenging life journeys. I trust that it will better enable us to realize God's high purpose in this life, which is the exciting process of being conformed to the image and likeness of Jesus Christ. As expressed by Paul, "And we, who with unveiled faces all reflect the Lord's glory, are being transformed into his likeness with ever-increasing glory, which comes from the Lord, who is the Spirit" (2 Cor 3:18 NIV). Finally, I pray that this book will enable us to journey faithfully and courageously to the end that we joyfully arrive at our eternal home.

I   *Initial Orientation*

Seeds of New Life

"Very truly I tell you, whoever
hears my word and believes him who
sent me has eternal life and . . .
has crossed over from death to life."

JOHN 5:24

After graduating from college and starting a job, Sharon, a friend of mine, experienced deep inner restlessness. She dabbled in spiritualism, and after a while she became heavily involved in the demonic world. Although claiming to be angels of light, the dark spirits were monstrous beyond description. They soon took control of her mind, resulting in the breakup of her marriage. Sharon sought help from the Unity church and other cult groups, but to no avail.

Now suicidal, she ran into a college friend—a Christian—who helped her see that Jesus Christ is stronger than the demonic spirits. Sharon responded positively to her friend's urging to surrender her life to the Savior, but the evil spirits continued to assail Sharon's mind with hateful and lustful thoughts. Seeking deliverance from the oppressive powers, she contacted an evangelical church in her town. The pastor invoked Christ's authority over her life and bade the evil spirits depart. Sharon was finally set free and able to begin her journey with Christ! Today Sharon has completed seminary, established a Christian ministry and has a powerful testimony for Christ.

NEW LIFE IN CHRIST

While not every story is as dramatic as Sharon's, every journey has a starting point, and the beginning of the Christian pilgrimage is decisive conversion to Jesus Christ. We can find conversion stories in Scripture, in church history, in contemporary writings and many other places.

> *"Christianity is not, in the long run, concerned either with individuals or communities . . . but with a new creature."*
>
> C. S. LEWIS

For example, the Old Testament character Ruth began her journey after her husband died. Rather than staying in her homeland of Moab, she traveled to Israel with her mother-in-law, Naomi, who had lost her husband and her sons. While Naomi encouraged Ruth to return to her family, Ruth pledged: "Where you go I will go, and where you stay I will stay. Your people will be my people and your God my God" (Ruth 1:16). Naomi's faithful witness brought Ruth, a pagan Moabitess, into the blessing of the Lord. Ruth's journey led her to marry Boaz and become part of the line of David and Jesus.

New Testament figure Saul of Tarsus was the son of a Pharisee and trained under the renowned Jewish teacher Gamaliel. By his own account Saul was "a Hebrew of the Hebrews; in regard to the law, a Pharisee; as for zeal, persecuting the church; as for righteousness based on the law, faultless" (Phil 3:5-6). Enraged that the new Christian movement posed a serious threat to Judaism, "Saul began to destroy the church. Going from house to house, he dragged off both men and women and put them in prison" (Acts 8:3). Later, "Saul was still breathing out murderous threats against the Lord's disciples" (Acts 9:1). The fanatical Pharisee gained authorization from the high priest to seize followers of Christ in Damascus and drag them back to Jerusalem in chains. As he approached the city, Saul encountered the risen Christ in the form of a brilliant light. Cast to the ground sightless, he surrendered his life to the One he was persecuting.

The conversion story of North African church father Augustine of Hippo (354-430) is another dramatic example of new life in Christ. Early in life he abandoned the Christian faith of his mother, Monica. For nearly a decade he embraced various forms of ancient philosophy. In his *Confessions* Augustine testified that his pre-Christian life was characterized by lying, stealing, lustful passions and other vices. One of his favorite pastimes was feasting his eyes on lewd theatrical shows. "Both [joy and lust] seethed together in hot confusion, and swept foolish youth over the precipice of passions that engulfed it in a whirlpool of shameful actions." At age seventeen he took a mistress with whom he had a son. During his teaching career at Rome and Milan he continued to live a life of moral recklessness, finding pleasure in doing what was forbidden. All the while Augustine was hungry for enduring truth and satisfying inner food, which he later recognized to be the triune God. Through the persistent prayers of his mother and the persuasive preaching of Jerome, bishop of Milan, Augustine drew closer to Christ.

As Augustine studied the Scriptures he slowly became reconciled intellectually to the truths of Christianity. Later, in the year 386, while struggling with the decision to follow Christ in the

privacy of his garden, he heard a child's voice repeating, "Take it,
read it! Take it, read it!" Augustine picked up the letters of the
apostle Paul and read the first words on which his eyes fell: "Not
in carousing and drunkenness, not in sexual immorality and de-
bauchery, not in dissension and jealousy. Rather, clothe yourself
with the Lord Jesus Christ, and do not think about how to gratify
the desires of the sinful nature" (Rom 13:13-14). Augustine testified, "No further did I desire to read, nor was there need. Indeed,
. . . all the darkness of doubt were dispersed, as if by a light of
peace flooding into my heart." After instruction in the faith Augustine was baptized by his mentor, Ambrose, was ordained to the
priesthood, and went on to serve as bishop of Hippo and as a pro-
lific writer of theology for more than thirty years.

C. S. Lewis, who died in 1963, trod a fascinating journey from
atheism to Romanticism to theism to faith in Christ. Lewis was
raised in a home that nominally adhered to the Church of England. The death of his mother at age ten led young Lewis to conclude that God was, if not cruel, at least a vague abstraction. Dis-
appointing experiences in boarding schools and the horrors of
World War I led Lewis to reject the idea of God's existence altogether. "I was at this time living, like so many Atheists or Anti-
theists, in a whirl of contradictions. I maintained that God did
not exist. I was also very angry with God for not existing. I was
equally angry with Him for creating a world." Later, as an Oxford
professor, Lewis struggled with more questions about God and
the meaning of life. Throughout his journey, however, the Spirit
was nurturing a deep longing in his heart. Influenced by Christian authors George MacDonald and G. K. Chesterton, as well as
by Christian friends such as J. R. R. Tolkien, Lewis at age thirty-
one exchanged atheism for theism. In his own words, "In the
Trinity Term of 1929 I gave in, and admitted that God was God,
and knelt and prayed: perhaps, that night, the most dejected and
reluctant convert in all England." Then, moving from intellectual

acceptance of God's existence to genuine Christianity, Lewis eventually committed his life to Jesus Christ.

A memorable conversion experience launched my own spiritual journey as well. My parents brought me as a child to a Bible-believing church near our New York home. From youth onward I sensed God convicting my heart about the need to surrender to Christ. Sunday after Sunday I resisted the Spirit's gentle invitation to welcome the Savior. Desiring to run my own life and make it big in the world, I left home for college in Pennsylvania. During my freshman year my heart was empty and unfulfilled. I returned to college early the second year for cross-country (running) practice; I was the only person in my dormitory. One evening the Holy Spirit came on me with enormous convicting power, prompting me to reach into my suitcase for the Bible my mother had placed there. Sitting at the top of the dormitory's circular staircase, I read the Scriptures until sunrise. At some early morning hour I gave my heart to Christ. When I next returned home I shared with my family my conversion experience. A dear aunt, long bedridden with illness, exclaimed, "Bruce, I have been praying since you were a babe that God would get hold of your life and use it for his glory."

These stories confirm that the spiritual journey begins with conversion to Jesus Christ by God's enabling grace. Though some Christians, nurtured from infancy in the church, may not recall the moment when they received new spiritual life, for many people entry into the Christian life is a conscious experience—a distinct moment of conversion.

DELIGHTS OF SALVATION

Christian salvation involves a radical transition from a life of sin to the life of grace—the unearned kindness and favor of God that makes salvation possible. When we are saved, we not only agree to the truth of the gospel but make a commitment to the person of Jesus Christ. By trusting Christ we come to the truth and pass from spiritual darkness into the light of Christ (1 Jn 1:5-7).

The Spirit also regenerates our hearts, making us new creations in Christ. "The old has gone, the new is here!" (2 Cor 5:17). Justified (made right with God) and regenerated (re-created as new persons), we are united with Christ. The triune God lives in us and we in him. In this spiritual union we die with Christ, putting an end to the mastery of sin in our lives. However, though we are complete in Christ, we continue to wrestle with sin throughout the journey—a reality Luther designated by the phrase "at one and the same time both righteous and a sinner." Thus begins the lifelong process of spiritual growth, or sanctification, which the Bible describes as putting off the "old self" and putting on the "new self" in Christ.

God graciously blesses us as believers with spiritual comforts that lead us to gratitude and praise. As we feel the deep changes of conversion inside us, we desire to know God more intimately. We are comforted by the fact that God has a purpose for our lives— restoration to Christlikeness that we might be the healing presence of the Savior in the world. We sense that God's plan for us is altogether "good, pleasing and perfect" (Rom 12:2).

The Scriptures provide enriching spiritual food to the new believer. Sweetness and pleasure well up in seasons of prayer as we discover that God hears and answers prayers. A deepening sense of God's unconditional love leads us to greater love for God. We gain a greater measure of the peace the Savior promised his followers as we cast our cares on Jesus. The child of God also experiences a growing sense of belonging within the community of believers.

Encouraged by these spiritual comforts, new Christians begin to seek to live a holy life pleasing to God (2 Cor 5:9). We also begin to discover our spiritual gifts and develop a vision of Christian life according to kingdom principles. We find purpose and satisfaction in serving others in Jesus' name. Recalling our own deliverance from sin, we develop a burden for the unsaved and in tentative ways begin to share our conversion story with others.

Early on the journey, new believers often experience considerable religious zeal. Nothing seems to matter more than knowing God and following him. As Thomas à Kempis observed, "How great is the fervor of new Christians right after joining the church! How great their devotion to prayer! What ambition to excel others in quality of life! How exact their discipline!"

John of the Cross summed up our experience as new Christians. "The soul, after it definitely converted to the service of God, is, as a rule, spiritually nurtured and caressed by God, even as is the tender child by its loving mother, who warms it with the heat of her bosom and nurtures it with sweet milk and soft and pleasant food, and carries it and caresses it in her arms."

STRUGGLE WITH THE FALLEN NATURE

Although God has declared us righteous in Christ, we retain our fallen nature, with its egotism and self-love. We desire to please God but often struggle against our old, sinful habits. Teresa of Ávila noted that the soul is like a garden full of weeds that need to be uprooted in order for it to grow. In our hearts we experience an inner warfare that at times can be intense. As expressed by Thomas à Kempis, "The old man, alas, yet lives within me. He has not yet been entirely crucified; he is not yet entirely dead. He still lusts strongly against the spirit, and he will not leave the kingdom of my soul in peace." Every Christian experiences this contest between old and new natures, but the warfare is particularly intense in those immature in the faith.

Biblical examples of spiritual struggle on the faith journey are plentiful:

> *"Our lives are a wonderful mixture of happiness and grief. We possess both our risen Lord Jesus Christ and the disastrous results of Adam's sin."*
>
> JULIAN OF NORWICH

- Noah was a man of faith, godly fear and obedience who "walked with God" (Gen 6:9). Yet drunkenness (Gen 9:21) reflects the spiritual conflict that divided Noah's heart.

- Abraham is described as a "friend of God" (2 Chron 20:7). Yet twice Abraham lied that his wife Sarah was his sister (Gen 12; 20), and failing to believe God's promise, he impatiently took Hagar as his concubine to bear a son (Gen 16).

- Jacob (the "supplanter") lied to Isaac and falsely seized the birthright blessing intended for Esau (Gen 27). Jacob later fathered children by several handmaidens of Rachel and Leah (Gen 30).

- David, a man after God's own heart, wrote seventy-three psalms of praise to God. Yet he committed adultery with Bathsheba and plotted the murder of her husband Uriah (2 Sam 11).

- Peter walked with Jesus for nearly three years. Yet he possessed multiple character deficiencies, including personal ambition, overconfidence, impulsiveness and shallowness of spiritual understanding.

CONTEMPORARY EXAMPLES

Along with the excitement and zeal of being a new Christian, believers also struggle with sinful passions. Lacking spiritual discipline, immature Christians may have to battle with destructive behaviors and habits.

A student of mine, whom I will call Ned, had a rough family background. His parents divorced when he was young, and his stepfather was an abusive alcoholic. By God's grace Ned became a Christian while serving in the Marine Corps, after which he enrolled in a state university. As a new believer he attended a weekend retreat sponsored by a Christian campus organization. Ned felt so empowered by the retreat experience that on returning home he impulsively challenged the devil to a duel. But his overconfidence quickly landed him in a dark pit of spiritual depression. In this weakened state, Ned cursed the Holy Spirit and later related to friends that he felt lost and damned. Fortunately, in spite of these highs and lows, Christians surrounded Ned with prayerful support and guided him to back to a more balanced place in his Christian walk.

A contrasting story, in which the fallen nature took control and brought on tragedy, took place in upscale Highlands Ranch, Colorado. Forty-one-year-old John Bishop lived there with his wife, Sherrill, and three beautiful children, ages six through nine. John and Sherrill were faithful churchgoers and Sunday school teachers. Family and neighbors regarded them as the ideal Christian couple. One evening after the family retired for the night, John removed a small caliber rifle from a closet and shot his sleeping wife. He then went to the children's rooms and shot them while they slept. The coroner determined that John was legally drunk at the time of the shootings. A deeply distraught family member said, "It was just despair on John's part." John's relationship with God had weakened of late, and he concluded in the face of certain trials that God was not actually there for him.

While John's experience is extreme, the truth is that we all have the forces of sin waging within us. With the old nature yet a potent force, as immature Christians we remain vulnerable to destructive spiritual powers greater than ourselves. Scripture offers some categories for the sin that we may confront in ourselves:

- arrogance (2 Cor 12:20)
- greed (1 Cor 5:10)
- envy (Gal 5:21)
- selfish ambition (Gal 5:20; Phil 2:3)
- jealousy (Gal 5:20)
- hatred (Gal 5:20)

- anger (2 Cor 12:20; Eph 4:31)
- lust (Col 3:5)
- love of money (1 Tim 6:9-10; Heb 13:5)

As young Christians we may also struggle with unrighteous behaviors that displease God, such as

- obscene talk (Eph 5:4)
- lying (Col 3:9)
- gossiping (2 Cor 12:20)
- cheating (1 Cor 6:8)
- stealing (1 Cor 6:9-10)
- drunkenness (Rom 13:13)
- sexual immorality (1 Cor 6:9-10)

Given the attention Scripture pays to it, sexual immorality, including homosexual behavior, is one of the more offensive manifestations of the old nature. Because we are made new in Christ, sexual sins—indeed, all other sins—must no longer enslave us as God's children. Nevertheless, our unguarded souls, through carelessness or inattention, may succumb once again to fleshly passions and ungodly behaviors.

A heart divided between the kingdom of God and the kingdom of this world cannot stand. To advance on the journey, we must allow the Spirit to put residual sin to death and strengthen the life of the Spirit within us.

ENTICEMENTS AND PLEASURES

Not yet firmly established in Christ, new believers remain drawn by the lure of worldly attractions, fascinated by things that can be seen, sensed and touched. Talk show host and author Dennis Prager put it well: "The human being is seduced by much that is ephemeral. If it glitters, we seek it. That this flaw is part of human nature is shown by the tale of the Garden of Eden." In his day Paul also recognized that some believers were earthly minded, "engrossed" in "the things of the world" (1 Cor 7:31). In this early stage of the journey, the glitter of fleeting, material stuff may prove stronger than the beauty of enduring, spiritual realities. Drawn to flashy things that offer little satisfaction, we may differ little from our non-Christian neighbors. We may believe the lie that our happiness depends on the quantity of material things we possess. Jesus warned against this mindset. "Watch out!" he taught, "life does not consist in an abundance of possessions" (Lk 12:15). "Nothing so mars and defiles the heart of man," Thomas à Kempis observed, "than impure attachment to created things."

As new believers we sometimes bring from our pre-Christian experience a love for fleeting pleasures that offer no lasting satisfaction. Early in the journey, there is a danger of being drawn away from spiritual treasures by these earthly, familiar pleasures. Through our indulgence in inordinate pleasures, we seek fulfillment apart from vital relationship with God. Freeing the soul from the worldly pleasures that once dominated our pre-Christian experience requires turning to God himself as our highest pleasure. As one of my favorite verses in the Bible puts it:

> *"It is your lack of interior pleasures that makes you go looking for exterior ones."*
>
> GUIGO I

You make known to me the path of life;
  you will fill me with joy in your presence,
  with eternal pleasures at your right hand. (Ps 16:11)

The appeal of worldly pleasures, possessions and honors results in a divided heart—torn between enticements of the sinful nature and loyalty to God. The heart so conflicted forfeits the peace God freely offers. François Fénelon, the French spiritual writer, observed that "new Christians give up their worst sins and break fewer laws than they once did, but they are still attached to the world. Instead of judging themselves by the Gospel they merely compare themselves with their former lives."

"We are deceived by five things we relish: riches, dignity, pleasure, power, and honors. These things chain us to sin and tie us up in faults."

RICHARD ROLLE

Though seated with Christ in heaven, the divided heart often walks the earth with the worldly and the profane. Considering the enticements of the world and its fleeting pleasures, young believers, at the beginning of the Christian life, must be intentional about turning from their old ways and wholeheartedly pursuing God.

KNOWING AND DOING

New believers face a number of other threats in the earliest stages of their faith. Immature Christians may focus more on *thinking* about God than truly *knowing* and *experiencing* God. Out of curiosity or perhaps pride, we may become engrossed with intellectual knowledge of divine things. But learning facts about God or the Bible, especially without love, offers no guarantee of deepening relationship with God. Christians young in the faith must be alert to the peril of intellectualism, in which we neglect the important relational and experiential dimensions of knowing. Young Christians, particularly, are susceptible to a dangerous split between the head and the heart. A seminary student struggling with intellectualism lamented: "I lack any real passion for God. My head is crammed with facts *about* God, while my heart is desperately hungry *for* God."

Seeking to please God, we may also fall into the trap of excessive activity—*doing* things for God rather than being in a transformative *relationship* with him. We try to earn God's favor by doing for him, but we fail to recognize that true discipleship involves far more than that. As young believers we may attempt to accomplish great things for God in our own strength. We may strive incessantly to prove our worth to self, others and even God himself. Even Christian work can become performance-driven and production-oriented rather than focusing on bringing glory to God. The life of the local church mistakenly can revolve around frenzied activities rather than authentic pursuit of God. In all this we march to the drum of our fast-paced, Western lifestyles that often leave us frazzled and numb. The American culture's emphasis on excessive working can seep into our spiritual life, leading us to put too much emphasis on doing for God rather than resting in knowing him and letting that relationship form us.

Remember Luke's story of maxed-out Martha when Jesus and his disciples visited for a meal. In the kitchen "Martha was distracted"—literally, overburdened—"by all the preparations that had to be made" (Lk 10:40). The demands of tidying the home, cooking the food and getting things just right for her guests rattled Martha. Frustrated, she wiped her hands with a towel, left the kitchen and chided Jesus for allowing Mary, her sister, simply to sit attentively focused on him. Martha was a woman of faith, but under the stress of inordinate activity she came apart. Permitting the pressures of service to overwhelm her, Martha succumbed to the tyranny of the urgent.

Believers readily admit to the burdens of excessive *doing*. A young seminarian comments, "My mind is full and my hands are busy, but my heart is empty and emotionally distant from God. Life moves so fast that God has become a blur." Likewise, a youth pastor testifies, "I have been doing ministry on a virtually empty tank, masking my immaturity and/or inferiority by accomplishing great things for the kingdom. I find myself on the West bank of the Jordan, unable to cross over to the Promised Land." A young woman reports: "My journey thus far has been based on performance. I know Christ as Savior and I say the right things around church, but I really do not know him well. I am frustrated, but keep up the show."

Excessive busyness fosters a sorrowful disconnect between the soul and God. A study of conservative Christians who left the church concluded that while most were busily engaged in activities, many were starving on the inside due to a lack of intimacy with God. We Christians have done reasonably well in the areas of knowing and doing, but poorly in the area of just *being*, or nurturing our inner world. British writer and poet Evelyn Underhill insightfully observed: "We mostly spend those lives conjugating three verbs—to Want, to Have, and to Do." But we forget "that none of these verbs have any ultimate significance, except so far as they are transcended by, and included in, the fundamental verb, to Be." The challenge facing young Christians is to live from the heart more intentionally, more reflectively and more prayerfully. Underhill added, "A certain slowing down and spacing out of our ceaseless clockwork activities is a necessary condition of the deepening and enriching of life. The spirit of Joy and the spirit of Hurry cannot live in the same house."

SPIRITUAL INFANCY AND ADOLESCENCE
Reflecting on an earlier phase of his journey, Paul wrote about the movement from childhood to adulthood in spiritual maturity (see 1 Cor 13:11). As spiritual novices we resemble a young child learning how to swim: first venturing into the shallows, then wading up to the waist, and finally jumping in to join other children at play. The young Christian's understanding of the faith is elementary, lacking mature knowledge of the Way.

After the first flush of enthusiasm, it's possible that our spiritual vitality may flatten out and become stale. In the face of difficulties or simply due to routine, spiritual sweetness may eventually dry up, instilling concern that the soul is not advancing. Some may be saddled with negative baggage from childhood or adolescence, such as a sense of unworthiness or mistrust of authority. Others may harbor a poor image of God, for example, as a strict disciplinarian intent on doing us in. Still others may believe the lie that God does not love them unconditionally with all their imperfections. Flagrant sins committed before becoming Christians—drug abuse, sexual immorality and the like—may burden the conscience. Some young believers may be unable to forgive themselves or receive God's forgiveness, resulting in yet another layer of guilt and shame. All of these issues can hinder growth and progress on the spiritual journey.

A young Christian related to me, "Three years after my conversion I find that I have drifted away from the spiritual glow I experienced when I came to know Christ. I'm unsure how to return to the path." Another a few years into the journey comments, "The terrain of my young Christian life has been as arduous as the Rocky Mountains, as disorienting as an endless desert, as delightful as a babbling brook and as lifeless as the Dead Sea."

Lacking knowledge, we may be uncertain how to grow our newfound faith. Failure to surrender to Christ's lordship may persist for some time. We may be like a young woman believer who admits, "I want God to put his stamp of approval on *my* plans." John of the Cross reminds us that "many of these beginners want God to desire what they want, and they become sad if they have to desire God's will." Not yet realizing the importance of the soul and the necessity of nurturing spiritual life, we

"No prolonged infancies among us, please. We'll not tolerate babes in the woods, small children who are an easy mark for imposters. God wants us to grow up, to know the whole truth and tell it in love—like Christ in everything."

EPH 4:14 *THE MESSAGE*

may be inconsistent in the practice of healthy spiritual habits or disciplines.

Prayers at this early stage may be superficial, consisting largely of requests for personal needs. On the other hand, a spirit of pride may occasionally develop regarding the practice of spiritual disciplines. We may not have learned how to listen well to the gentle whispers of the Spirit. A young Christian comments, "I spend little time listening to God for fear of what He might say to me. I enjoy controlling my life, and if I listen God might challenge that control." Uncertain how to respond appropriately to the Spirit's leading, we may make unwise decisions and wander from the path. Or we may fail to act decisively when God has made clear the way.

It's essential for new believers to establish a clear identity in Christ. Otherwise, our sense of self may be shaped by who others say we are rather than how God sees us. We may have heard condemning messages from the father of lies rather than the heavenly Father's affirmation of our status as dearly beloved in Christ. Low self-esteem and self-rejection may gnaw at our souls and weaken our pursuit of God. Craving affirmation of worth, we may seek the approval and applause of peers. Uncomfortable with intimacy, we may hold God and others at arm's length, and so remain hidden. As James chided believers of his day, "You're spoiled children, each wanting your own way" (Jas 4:3 *The Message*).

Early on the journey many find themselves *doing* church without *being* church. One believer young in the faith commented, "Church is something you 'did'; there was little experience of community." He added, "My early Christian experience consisted merely of 'showing up' when the doors of the church were open. I didn't serve, worship or participate; I just showed up. I believed that 'showing up' was all that was required." Doing church is a poor substitute for engaging relationship with Jesus Christ, the head of the church.

Paul described the spiritual state of many immature Christians of his day as "tossed back and forth by the waves, and blown here and there by every wind of teaching and by the cunning and craftiness of people in their deceitful scheming" (Eph 4:14).

In his classic work *The Dark Night of the Soul,* John of the Cross identified common imperfections of spiritual beginners in the form of seven capital sins that must be remedied in order to advance on the journey:

- spiritual pride with respect to one's achievements
- spiritual avarice prompted by dissatisfaction with God's blessings
- spiritual luxury prompted by dissatisfaction with God's blessings
- bitterness and anger, experienced when spiritual satisfaction fades
- spiritual gluttony, or the quest for pleasure and consolation in spiritual exercises
- spiritual envy, or coveting the accomplishments of others
- spiritual sloth, or acedia, where one wearies at the demands of discipleship, and slackens zeal

John concluded that beginners "resemble children who kick and cry and struggle to walk by themselves when their mothers want to carry them; in walking by themselves they make no headway, or if they do, it is at a child's pace." He described the early phase of the journey as a life of fascination with the pleasures of sense. He intended that his harsh description of the novice's spiritual life would "help beginners understand the feebleness of their state" and "how very similar their deeds are to those of children." His critique sounds harsh, but he ultimately sought to stimulate young Christians to progress on the journey.

If, as new Christians, we're not intentional about pressing forward on the path, we could get stuck in an immature spiritual state. George Barna indicates that only half of evangelical Christians possess a plan for spiritual growth, and that many who do have a plan achieve unsatisfactory outcomes. Without firm resolve we falter along the way. The Barna organization conducted a spiritual maturity survey of 1,008 adults. "The data show that millions of people who are aligned with the Christian faith have not thought very much or very clearly about what spiritual maturity means." In addition, "Most people do not know what faith maturity looks like." Dallas Willard comments that many Christians live lives of quiet desperation. I understand such a statement to mean that many believers know they need to mature as disciples of Jesus, but they are frustrated by their inability to get there. Many professing Christians remain "mere infants in Christ" (1 Cor 3:1).

"We are too occupied with our own whims and fancies, too taken up with passing things. Rarely do we completely conquer even one vice, and we are not inflamed with the desire to improve ourselves day by day; hence, we remain cold and indifferent."

THOMAS À KEMPIS

ADDITIONAL DANGERS AND THREATS

New believers face many perils. Because their new spiritual life does not yet have a well-established foundation, new Christians must be alert to some of the dangers and threats inherent in immature faith.

Well intentioned, we may fall into the trap of legalism—a morality-based system that believes life is governed by a strict code of rules or dos and don'ts. Seeking to earn God's favor by living virtuously, we may drift into the joyless bondage of law-keeping. We sing lines of the hymn, "Free from the law, O happy condition, Jesus has bled and there is remission," but we may find ourselves slavishly following a code of regulations. Such a works-based right-eousness readily morphs into a self-righteousness that is critical and unforgiving of others. This legalistic mindset opposes the rule of love enjoined by Jesus and his apostles. Where legalism prevails, freedom in Christ remains an elusive ideal.

Young Christians can also fall into the trap of perfectionism (not to be confused with the legitimate pursuit of excellence). Lacking a realistic sense of self-worth, or because of an overbearing upbringing, the perfectionist believes that his or her value is contingent on impeccable performance. Christ's command "Be perfect" (Mt 5:48) does not mean that we achieve sinlessness but that we realize wholeness or maturity. However, the perfectionist lacks self-acceptance and instead lives under false guilt, self-loathing and perhaps addictive behaviors. All of this results in slower spiritual progress. Perfectionist Christians must understand that by faith we are clothed in Christ's perfect righteousness and thus fully accepted as the beloved.

"We must keep our guard up. Satan will try to turn our minds and hearts away from God by making us think we can have or do something more valuable."

FRANCIS OF ASSISI

In addition to the dangers of legalism and perfectionism, new believers face the risk of ignorance of spiritual warfare dynamics. Being immature, we are vulnerable to the wiles of the devil. The evil one

- stalks saints (1 Pet 5:8)
- deceives the mind (Gen 3:13)
- leads people astray (Rev 12:9)
- works counterfeit miracles (2 Thess 2:9)
- incites to sin (Acts 5:3)

Calvin summed up Satan's seductions this way: "An enemy relentlessly threatens us, an enemy who is the very embodiment of rash boldness, of military prowess, of crafty wiles, of untiring zeal and haste, of every conceivable weapon and of skill in the science of warfare." We often are ignorant of how the world and the devil conspire with the flesh to incite our hearts to sin. We may fail to discern the truth that "our struggle is not against flesh and blood, but against the rulers, against the authorities, against the powers of this dark world and against the spiritual forces of evil in the heavenly realms" (Eph 6:12).

In seasons of testing or suffering we may be tempted to turn from the path of discipleship and revisit the old life. By slackening commitment we may backslide for a season. We may even rebel against God and choose to follow Satan. Chafing at the cost of following Christ, those who are immature in the faith might be tempted to embrace an alternative path—an Eastern religion, the New Age or the occult. Recent research reveals that a growing number of younger adults are withdrawing from committed Christian living.

King Solomon is a prime example of a backslidden believer. When Solomon loved and obeyed God, "the LORD his God was with him and made him exceedingly great" (2 Chron 1:1). Later, however, Solomon married seven hundred women and had three hundred concubines, with disastrous results. "As Solomon grew old, his wives turned his heart after other gods, and his heart was not fully devoted to the LORD his God" (1 Kings 11:4).

Another example of backsliding is Demas, an associate of Paul who aided the apostle during his imprisonment in Rome. Paul later testified, "Demas, because he loved this world, has deserted me and gone to Thessalonica" (2 Tim 4:10). Backsliding must not be confused with apostasy, which is the willful repudiation of the good news. Immature Christians must heed the warning issued by Paul: "So, if you think you are standing firm, be careful that you don't fall!" (1 Cor 10:12).

MOVING FORWARD

Deciding for Christ is only the beginning of the life of discipleship and spiritual formation. Far more than getting our ticket to heaven stamped, conversion is an ongoing process of allowing the Spirit to put sin to death and initiate transformation of every dimension of our lives. Ongoing conversion through daily acts of repentance and faith is crucial throughout the journey, especially due to the number of dangers and threats to a young faith. In the spiritual life instant maturity is an oxymoron. Replacing works of the flesh with the fruit of the Spirit occurs over time with much discipline and prayer. Aligning mind, will, emotions and actions with those of Christ represents the challenging task of a lifetime.

As a mother lovingly nurtures her newborn, so God relentlessly pursues transformation of his children into the image of his Son that they might serve him well in the world. C. S. Lewis observed, "Every Christian is to become a little Christ. The whole purpose of becoming a Christian is simply nothing else." To mature on the journey, we must surrender to God, resist the seductions of Satan and practice time-honored disciplines of spiritual formation. Putting on Christ likely requires being formed by the refining fires of trials and suffering. The church father John Chrysostom observed that in order to reach the Promised Land one must inevitably pass through the desert. How God pursues this goal will be addressed in chapters to follow.

"Since the condition of beginners in the way of God is lowly and not too distant from love of pleasure and self . . . God desires to withdraw them from this base manner of loving and lead them on to a higher degree of divine love."

JOHN OF THE CROSS

FOR INDIVIDUAL OR GROUP REFLECTION
AND DISCUSSION

1. As you ponder your early Christian experience, what were your significant delights, blessings and comforts? On the other hand, identify those spiritual deficits and desolations that once troubled you.

2. How characteristic of your life are the imperfections that John of the Cross, in *The Dark Night of the Soul*, identified in beginners (p. 33)? In other words, what are the most important spiritual formation issues you are currently engaged with?

3. Ponder the extent to which you currently struggle with legalism, perfectionism or performance-based living.

4. Have you ever seriously been tempted to abandon discipleship and return to a more predictable and comfortable way of life? What was that experience like?

2 *Painful Disorientation*

Seasons of Distress

"In all this you greatly rejoice,
though now for a little while you
may have had to suffer grief
in all kinds of trials."

1 PETER 1:6

A friend of mine, whom I will call Cheryl, was married to a counseling graduate of a leading seminary. Her husband, whom I will call Mark, pastored two churches over nine years. During their marriage Cheryl gradually realized that Mark was a people pleaser who refused to accept responsibility, and in his second pastorate Mark neglected his relationship with God, drifted to the left theologically and began to "sleep around." Having backslid, Mark withdrew from the ministry and bailed out of the marriage,

leaving Cheryl and their three children financially destitute. Emotionally distraught, she cried out to heaven, "Why, God, when I
faithfully follow you, have you allowed this to happen?" Confused
and distressed, Cheryl entertained real doubts about God's care
for her and the children. Through the tears she questioned, *Do I
really want to stay with Jesus? Can I trust him with my life and family?* Cheryl's experience shows that even dedicated Christians suffer seasons of painful distress.

PEACHES AND CREAM?

When I faced a hardship as a child, my mother encouraged me
with the down-to-earth counsel, "Life is not all peaches and
cream." A *Peanuts* cartoon similarly
targets the issue: Charlie Brown and
Lucy are reflecting together on life's
difficult or puzzling moments. Charlie thoughtfully comments to Lucy,
"Life has its ups and downs." Pondering this, Lucy replies, "Charlie,
why can't life just have its ups and
ups?"

> *"The quest of the modern*
> *Christian is likely to be for*
> *peace of mind and spiritual joy,*
> *with a good degree of*
> *material prosperity thrown in*
> *as an external proof of the*
> *divine favor."*
>
> A. W. TOZER

There's a twisted version of the
gospel that asserts that God intends
Christians' lives to always be on the
up and up. The so-called prosperity
gospel—also known as the "health-
and-wealth gospel" or the "name-it-and-claim-it theology"—
insists that God wills material prosperity, perfect health and a
trial-free life for everyone who claims these in faith. Many followers of Jesus, prosperity advocates assert, possess little and suffer
much because of deficient faith. A popular preacher exhorted his
large congregation, "God wants you to get the best deals in life,"
adding, "You have a right to preferential treatment, to special ad-

vantages." Thousands of undiscerning Christians flock to hear slick purveyors of the prosperity message. C. S. Lewis, however, claimed the very opposite. "Prosperity knits a person to the World. He feels that he is 'finding his place in it,' while really it is finding its place in him."

The notion that the good life is free from distress and suffering reflects society's pursuit of comfort and aversion to pain. We all naturally seek a life free of hardship and suffering. When we encounter disappointment or distress we ask, *Why is this happening to me?* Or perhaps, *Why has God failed me?* But the journey to Christian maturity rarely navigates through smooth seas. Though we long for fair skies and gentle breezes, we often get thunderclouds and hurricane winds. In a fallen world, humanity's lot is one of distress and suffering.

LIFE'S INEVITABLE TRIALS

All humans at one time or another experience disappointments, chronic illnesses and misfortunes of various sorts. Disability, divorce and death are painfully embedded in the human experience. Anguished images of the World Trade Center on 9/11, the war in Iraq and hurricane Katrina are engraved in our memory banks. The Russian writer Fyodor Dostoyevsky simply asserted, "To live is to suffer." Millennia earlier a wise man mused:

> Trouble doesn't come from nowhere.
> It's human! Mortals are born and bred for trouble,
>   as certainly as sparks fly upward. (Job 5:6-7 *The Message*)

The apostle Peter alerted scattered saints that the journey involves trials, persecutions and suffering. Thomas à Kempis noted that "absolute security and peace do not exist in this world," adding, "so long as we live in this world we have trouble and temptation." The human family suffers because we are fallen creatures living this side of Eden.

Neither are Jesus' followers immune from distress. As sheep in a world of wolves, friends of Jesus experience physical, emotional and spiritual hardship just like everyone else. Often when life seems to be going great—when we are most committed and productive—we hit major road bumps that challenge our spiritual stability. Sooner or later, the comforts we experienced early on the journey give way to feelings of desolation. The fourth-century monk Pseudo-Macarius put it well: "Where the Holy Spirit is, there follows, as a shadow, persecution and struggle." The history of the church brings painful reminders of apparent misfortune, from the stoning of Stephen to the martyrdom of missionaries in our day.

"What does anyone know who doesn't know how to suffer for Christ?"

JOHN OF THE CROSS

Sometimes Christians are even targeted with increased hardship because of their faith. On April 29, 1999, two enraged students smuggled guns and bombs into Columbine High School, located three miles from our home in Littleton, Colorado, killing twelve students and a teacher. One attacker pointed a gun at student Cassie Bernall and asked, "Do you believe in God?" When Cassie, a courageous Christian, replied, "Yes, I believe in God," he shot her in the head.

From painful experience David testified, "Many are the afflictions of the righteous" (Ps 34:19 NRSV). Jesus reminded his followers, "In this world you will have trouble" (Jn 16:33)—the word for *trouble* in the original language of the Bible means "oppression, affliction, tribulation." Although his righteous life was well pleasing to the Father, Jesus himself experienced suffering both in life and in death. Paul reminded the church at Philippi, "For it has been granted to you on behalf of Christ not only to believe on him, but also to suffer for him" (Phil 1:29). Disappointment, suffering and betrayal frequently assail us all on our homeward journeys.

DESTABILIZING THE SOUL

An unexpected disappointment, a serious illness or a major life crisis can leave even Christians emotionally distressed and weakened. Walter Brueggemann describes this disorientation as "a churning, disruptive experience of dislocation"—or more grievously, as an experience "of being overwhelmed, nearly destroyed." We who faithfully represent Jesus in the world may be overcome with confusion, helplessness or dread when we are going through hard times. In this condition we may cry out with David, "My spirit grows faint within me; / my heart within me is dismayed" (Ps 143:4).

Disorienting experiences highlight how fragile we humans are and how desperately we need to grow strong in the Lord. The greater our suffering and pain, the more the sinful flesh is being cut away. Through life's distressing seasons God gets our attention and points out a better path to maturity and fruitfulness. Immature saints early on the journey are like wild colts needing to be broken and trained; through trying times, God lovingly breaks us in order to retrain and reform us. While we still experience God's presence, these situations of crisis and emptiness both test and stress our relationship with God.

Military trainers pursue a similar strategy of breaking and remaking the human psyche. By rigorous discipline, branches of the armed services seek to strip the recruit of his or her persona in order to rebuild a new identity as a disciplined and brave warrior. Because we are stubbornly rooted in selfishness, we need discipline to come to the end of our ropes, trust God fully and be transformed. James wrote, "Consider it pure joy, my brothers and sisters, whenever you face trials of many kinds, because you know that the testing of your faith produces perseverance. Let perseverance finish its work so that you may be mature and complete, not lacking anything" (Jas 1:2-4).

EXPERIENCED BY OLD-COVENANT SOULS

Scripture records the journeys of many of God's servants who experienced affliction, desolation and even moments of despair. Consider a few examples.

Job was an upright man who shunned evil (Job 1:1). Yet God permitted Satan to assault him, depriving righteous Job of his possessions, servants, ten children and health. So intense was Job's physical and emotional suffering that his wife urged him to curse God and die. The remainder of the book portrays Job pleading his innocence, searching for answers and railing against God. Powerful emotions—discouragement, bitterness, cynicism, even anger—overwhelmed his soul. Earlier in his ordeal Job said, "God you owe me answers!" and during his painful journey he questioned, "Why is this happening to me?" But humbled and refined by his trials, Job gained deeper understanding of God (although in no way fully comprehending the mystery of God's ways).

"God is frequently closer to us in sickness than in health. . . . When pains come from God, only He can heal them. Sometimes a disease of the body will cure a sickness of the soul."

BROTHER LAWRENCE

Though he was "a man after [God's] own heart" (1 Sam 13:14), David experienced years of trouble. He was often hiding or on the run because Saul repeatedly plotted to kill him. Later he sunk into a pit of guilt-ridden despair when he committed adultery with Bathsheba and plotted the death of her husband, Uriah (2 Sam 11). The son David fathered with Bathsheba died as punishment for his deeds of adultery and murder. As if that were not enough, David's son Absalom rebelled against him and drove him out of Jerusalem. Trouble continued to plague David's extended family as Amnon, David's first son, raped his half-sister Tamar. In an act of revenge Absalom murdered Amnon, rebelled against his father and slept with his father's wives. All this fulfilled God's prediction, "Out of your own household I am going to bring calamity on you" (2 Sam 12:11).

Other biblical examples of spiritual and emotional trials include:

• Abraham was a man to whom God promised to give a male heir through Sarah (Gen 15:4). Yet without explanation, God commanded the godly patriarch to offer his treasured son Isaac on an altar of stones as a human sacrifice (Gen 22).

• Joseph was cast into a muddy cistern by his jealous brothers and sold as a slave in a foreign land (Gen 37). Later, Joseph was sexually propositioned by Potiphar's wife and thrown into prison (Gen 39:20) for a crime he never committed.

• The Israelites were forced into harsh slave labor in Egypt. A pharaoh commanded that all newborn males be killed (Ex 1:16) and later that every male child be drowned in the Nile (Ex 1:22). As the psalmist recalled, God "passed us like silver through refining fires, . . . / pushed us to our very limit . . . / [and] took us to hell and back" (Ps 66:10-12 *The Message*). Following miraculous deliverance through the Red Sea, the Israelites wandered for forty years in the desert, where their lot was one of hunger, thirst, idolatry, punishment and divine encounter.

• After his miraculous victory over 850 false prophets on Mount Carmel, Elijah was threatened by Jezebel, then fled into the wilderness, overcome with fatigue, self-pity and depression. The prophet crawled under a bush and prayed that he might die. " 'I have had enough, LORD,' he said. 'Take my life; I am no better than my ancestors' " (1 Kings 19:4).

• Jeremiah, the weeping prophet who preached judgment on Judah, stood alone, betrayed by his own family (Jer 12:6). The man of God was arrested, beaten and consigned to a dungeon.

After being released from prison the fearless preacher was thrown into a cistern to starve (Jer 38:9). "Why is my pain unending and my wound grievous and incurable?" (Jer 15:18), God's faithful spokesman asked.

ENGAGED BY NEW-COVENANT PEOPLE

Our Lord Jesus himself lived a life of hardship, rejection and ultimately death on a cross. In Gethsemane Jesus found himself in an agonizing spiritual crisis. When the Lord entered the garden with his three disciples "he began to be sorrowful and troubled" (Mt 26:37). In stronger language still Mark states that Jesus "began to be deeply distressed or troubled" (Mk 14:33). The word translated "deeply distressed" means "overcome with terror." *The Message* version of this verse reads, Jesus "plunged into a sinkhole of dreadful agony."

Knowing what lay before him, Jesus shared his agony with his three friends. "My soul is overwhelmed with sorrow to the point of death" (Mt 26:38). So intense was Jesus' anguish in prayer that sweat ran down his face like drops of blood. The harsh reality is that "Jesus came [to Gethsemane] to be with the Father for an interlude before his betrayal, but found hell rather than heaven opened before him, and he staggered."

Then there was Simon Peter. Jesus' arrest and trials placed all of Peter's beliefs about God's plan in jeopardy. Cautiously, Peter entered the courtyard of the high priest, warming himself by a fire. When a servant girl noted that Peter had been with Jesus, the disciple said, "I don't know what you're talking about" (Mt 26:70). A second identified Peter as one of Jesus' followers, which Peter vigorously denied with an oath: "I don't know the man!" (Mt 26:72). Other bystanders, alerted by his Galilean accent, identified him as a companion of Jesus. Calling down curses on himself if his words were false, Peter again replied, "I don't know the man!" (Mt 26:74). Denial, denial with an oath and denial with curses on himself!

Immediately a rooster crowed, and the disciple who vowed never to fail his Lord recalled Jesus' prediction of his denial. Shattered to the core, Peter stumbled out of the courtyard and wept. When Jesus passed by, his sorrow-filled eyes met Peter's eyes, causing the latter to become overwhelmed with a deep sense of failure. When Jesus staggered up the path to Calvary in disgrace, Peter remained in hiding. Later, after Peter heard the details of Jesus' gruesome crucifixion, he must have sunk into an even deeper pit of gloom.

"To do His supreme work of grace within you He will take from your heart everything you love most. Everything you trust in will go from you. Piles of ashes will lie where your most precious treasures used to be."

A. W. TOZER

Other examples of suffering saints include the following:

- John the Baptist. When the Baptist confronted Herod with his adulterous marriage to Herodias, his brother's ex-wife, Herodias determined to kill him. John was arrested, bound and thrown in prison. When Herodias's daughter asked for John's head on a platter, Herod ordered the Baptist beheaded (Mk 6:21-28).

- Apostle Paul. On his mission journeys Christianity's greatest missionary experienced trials, sufferings, life-threatening hardships, persecutions, shipwrecks, beatings and imprisonment. Paul also struggled with a painful but unspecified "thorn in my flesh, a messenger of Satan, to torment me" (2 Cor 12:7). God in his loving wisdom chose to not to remove Paul's distressing "thorn."

- First-century believers also bore much travail. The Master's followers suffered manifold hardships, unsettling trials, fiery ordeals, insults and persecutions. For two thousand years since, Christians have at times been imprisoned, tortured and killed.

In the twentieth century more disciples have been martyred for Christ than in the previous two millennia of church history. In our day churches are still burned and Christians tortured in many countries, such as North Korea, Vietnam, China, Pakistan and the Sudan.

The sufferings endured by godly people in Scripture and throughout history serve as examples for us as Jesus' apprentices today. Reflecting on his own times, Pseudo-Macarius claimed that sufferings "show that the power of divine grace . . . and the gift of the Holy Spirit which is given to the faithful soul come forth with much contention, with much endurance, patience, trials and testings."

DISORIENTATION IN CHRISTIAN HISTORY

As further evidence that our lot as believers often is one of hardship and suffering, consider the struggles experienced by leading Christians from the past.

John Bunyan (1628-1688), author of *Grace Abounding to the Chief of Sinners* and *Pilgrim's Progress*, was a popular Baptist preacher who encountered many trials throughout his life. At age sixteen both his mother and sister died. Young Bunyan suffered from depression to the point of contemplating suicide. His first wife, Mary, and their sightless daughter succumbed to fever. When Charles II ascended the throne, the freedom that separatist Christians enjoyed for two decades ended, and in 1660 Bunyan was imprisoned for preaching without a license. For twelve years he languished in the disease-ridden Bedford jail, distressed at being forcefully separated from his wife and four children. Bunyan wrote, "The parting . . . hath oft been to me in this place as the pulling the flesh from my bones," adding, "I have been in my spirit so filled with darkness, that I could not so much conceive what that God and that comfort was with which I have been refreshed." When the Declaration of Indulgence was published Bunyan was released, but he was imprisoned again for six months when persecution against separatists was renewed.

Raised in a devout home, Corrie Ten Boom (1892-1983) trusted Christ at age five. In 1944 when the Germans learned that the Ten Boom family was sheltering Jews, the Gestapo sent them to prison, where Corrie's father died ten days later. Corrie herself was placed in solitary confinement with only the barest of rations. Corrie and her sister, Betsie, were interrogated and physically beaten, yet Corrie faithfully shared Christ's love with her captors.

After four months Corrie and her sister were transferred to the Ravensbrück concentration camp, where they were housed with fourteen hundred other prisoners in a barracks designed to hold four hundred people. Betsie died shortly after arriving, despite Corrie's heroic efforts to keep her alive. Daily Corrie heard the sounds of firing squads, observed the smoke pouring from the crematoria and feared that soon she would be sent to the gas chamber. As a result of an administrative error, Corrie was released on December 31, 1944. Within a week of her discharge all the women of her age group were killed. In the years that followed Corrie suffered three strokes that crippled her ability to speak; nevertheless she continued to intercede for the world.

Other leading Christians who suffered in various ways include:

- Augustine (354-430). The leading churchman and theologian became deeply distraught when his son, Adeodatus, died of a strange illness. Augustine then wrestled with how a loving God could take the life of his beloved son and questioned many beliefs he formerly held dear. Through these trials God was summoning his servant to a place of complete surrender.

- Teresa of Ávila (1515-1582). In her Carmelite monastery Teresa became so sick that preparations were made for her burial. After recovering, she suffered a three-year paralysis that left her unable to walk, and she later suffered from both malaria and arthritis. When revival broke out in the order under her leadership, opponents reported her to the Roman Inquisition to purge what was interpreted as a challenge to established orthodoxy.

- David Brainerd (1718-1747). David's parents died when he was a young boy. At Yale, where he contracted the measles and tuberculosis, Brainerd was expelled from the college when he severely criticized a professor who opposed the Great Awakening. As a missionary to Native Americans he lived alone in the wilderness, suffering from loneliness, physical ailments, absence of apparent ministry success and episodes of depression.

- Friedrich von Hügel (1852-1925). The Austrian-born spiritual director and writer suffered from typhus that left him frail and nearly deaf. His eldest daughter, Gertrude, died at age thirty-eight. Reflecting on his sickly condition and loss, Hügel wrote, "All deepened life is deepened suffering." Contrary to expectations, "God does not make our lives all shipshape, clear, and comfortable."

- Amy Carmichael (1867-1951). Ministering in India for fifty-five years rescuing needy children and young women from temple prostitution and the injustices of the caste system, Amy suffered throughout her life from the chronic pain of neuralgia, as well as from dengue fever, depression, opposition from the authorities and satanic attacks. Falling into a pit at age sixty-four, she suffered a broken leg and spinal injury, causing her to remain largely bedridden for the final twenty years of her life.

"I found myself so constricted on every side that the only remedy I discovered was to raise my eyes to heaven and call upon God."

TERESA OF ÁVILA

Our overview of Scripture and Christian history indicates that many prominent Christians suffered from trials that providentially came their way. God accomplishes his most profound work in the lives of his children not in times of tranquility but in seasons of hardship. According to spiritual writer Jean Pierre de Caussade, "God instructs the heart, not through ideas but through suffering and adversity."

AFFLICTION HITS HOME

The suffering I've experienced in my own life has taught me a number of important lessons. As I was writing this book, unexpected lower back pain led surgeons to recommend lumbar fusion surgery. While in the hospital for this operation, I contracted a staph infection and shortly after was also diagnosed with a hernia that required surgery.

For two decades I have managed with Menieres disease, a condition where fluid pressure builds up in an inner ear causing periodic dizziness and vertigo attacks. Recent medical treatment and two previous surgeries appeared to have stabilized the problem, but the four-and-a-half hours under anesthesia for the back surgery reactivated my Menieres symptoms. For several months this treatment itself caused debilitating side effects that included dizziness and nausea.

During the course of a few months, then, I suffered pain and fatigue from major back surgery, a chemical surgery on the inner ear and hernia surgery. I languished physically and emotionally, comparing myself with suffering Job. During this season of struggle I wrestled with God, asking, "Why, God, have you allowed this anguish to come my way?" I believe that God responded to my questioning by saying that although I had been writing about seasons of distress and disorientation, now he was going to put me through the same so that I would understand suffering not merely intellectually but experientially. Isn't it like God, I thought, to work in such an unexpected way in our lives?

I have learned through this ordeal lessons that could not be otherwise learned, such as the fleeting nature of life, our need for

people, empathy for others who are hurting and deepened trust in
God. I have learned that the Father relentlessly works to reshape
his blood-bought children into the likeness of his Son.

REDEMPTIVE OUTCOMES OF TRIALS AND AFFLICTIONS

A radio preacher recently claimed that since Christ has conquered
every evil power, suffering has no purpose in Christians' lives.
Posing the question, "What should we do when we suffer?" he
urged, "Find a way out of the suffer-
ing." Of course, obstacles and afflictions have the potential to break
people's spirits, leading to loss of
hope and despair. The preacher's
prescription, however, misses some
important truths: Human suffering
is an inescapable fact of life as a fruit
of the Fall into disobedience and sin.
Moreover, God often uses the hard-
ships and pain life brings our way to mature us. Hügel rightly insisted, "Suffering is the greatest teacher . . . and . . . the crown of
life." He offered the counsel, "Plant yourself on foundations that
are secure—God—Christ—Suffering—the Cross."

"Sweet are the uses of adversity,

Which like the toad, ugly and venomous,

Weave yet a precious jewel in his head."

WILLIAM SHAKESPEARE

Although we cannot understand the depths of God's mysterious
purposes, distresses can become the source of greater blessing. Let's
explore some redemptive outcomes of the crosses we bear.

Hardship and suffering can enhance self-knowledge, offering
insight into our imperfections. Often we don't know what we are
made of until we're pushed to the wall. Adversity strengthens
character, building qualities such as humility, patience, fortitude
and trust. When our faith is tested, we have the opportunity to
develop spiritual character as we persevere through turbulent
storms. Paul testified to the character-building value of suffering:
"We know that suffering produces perseverance; perseverance,

character; and character, hope" (Rom 5:3-4).

That hardship strengthens character is illustrated by the life cycle of a butterfly. The butterfly beats its wings against the walls of its cocoon in order to break free from its encasement. If someone were to assist the butterfly's escape by forcing a hole in its cocoon, the butterfly would not have gained the strength necessary to survive, and so it would die.

A few years ago world-class cyclist Lance Armstrong was diagnosed with testicular cancer, which metastasized to other organs. Expert medical treatment and courageous determination on his part sent the life-threatening cancer into remission. During a national television appearance promoting the Lance Armstrong Foundation, he squarely confronted his enemy. "Cancer, you made me what I am today. Cancer, you made me smarter, more determined, and a believer in miracles."

Distressing afflictions loosen sin's grip on our lives. Heartwrenching trials break our stubborn wills, purge our sinful passions and amend our shameful behaviors. As fire purifies gold from the dross, as juice is pressed from grapes and as a vine is pruned of dead branches, so affliction has the potential to refine the soul. The psalmist mused, "Before I was afflicted I went astray" (Ps 119:67). Peter reckoned that "those who have suffered in their bodies are done with sin" (1 Pet 4:1). And even Paul dealt with his "thorn in the flesh." William Tyndale, the English reformer, testified: "The Holy Spirit uses tribulation to purge us, to kill our fleshly wit, our worldly understanding. . . . Then we can be filled with the wisdom of God."

Seasons of distress can deepen our relationship with God. We die to self-love more readily in difficult rather than in comfortable times. When life goes smoothly we tend to rely on our own resources. But when life caves in we turn to the God whom we instinctively know is our only help. We pursue God when the pain of remaining unchanged is greater than the effort needed to change and grow. John Calvin declared, "The more we are afflicted with adversities, the more surely our fellowship with Christ is confirmed!" Calamities can either draw us nearer to God or drive us further from him. The difference lies with our response.

Suffering also cultivates empathy for the misfortunes of others. Whose heart bleeds more over the death of a child than one who has lost a son or daughter? Who can feel the despair of a cancer patient better than one who has suffered with cancer? Who experiences the distress of a failed marriage more than an abandoned spouse? The apostle Paul developed the gift of empathy as a result of his afflictions. He praised "the Father of compassion and the God of all comfort, who comforts us in all our troubles, so that we can comfort those in any trouble with the comfort we ourselves receive from God" (2 Cor 1:3-4). As we empathize with the trials of others, we discover that our troubles often pale in comparison.

"People find it very hard to believe that God heaps crosses on those he loves. . . . But though God could save us without crosses, he has not willed to do so, just as he has willed that men should grow up through weakness and troubles of childhood, instead of being born fully developed men."

FRANÇOIS FÉNELON

God often turns calamities into opportunities for kingdom advancement. Following the 1999 shootings at Columbine High School, my wife and I walked through the adjacent Clement Park with Bible in hand. People were sobbing, and scores of hastily erected memorials displayed Scripture texts and comforting spiritual sayings. Seventy-five thousand people flocked to an outdoor memorial service at which Franklin Graham preached. For weeks local congregations were packed with citizens stunned by the tragedy. A Denver television station reported, "The professional counsel-

ing community is pouring into Littleton, but the kids are flocking
to the churches." Following the Columbine horror a mini-revival
broke out as the tragedy put life in perspective and led many people to trust in Christ.

Although we naturally resist suffering, God sometimes accomplishes his most important work in our lives through it. C. S.
Lewis learned firsthand that distress often proves to be a "severe
mercy." James wrote, "Consider it a sheer gift, friends, when tests
and challenges come at you from all sides. You know that under
pressure, your faith-life is forced into the open and shows its true
colors. So don't try to get out of anything prematurely. Let it do its
work so you become mature and well-developed, not deficient in
any way" (Jas 1:2-4 *The Message*). Fénelon, the spiritual writer,
noted, "The world says, 'How terrible for those who suffer!' But
from the depths of my heart faith replies, 'How terrible for the
world when it does *not* suffer!' "

The popular opinion that sin is the immediate cause of all suffering dies slowly. Job's three well-intentioned comforters erred in
giving this opinion. As we have seen, some of the most saintly
souls have been the most afflicted. In his wisdom God often turns
up the heat when he sees gold worth purifying. John Wycliffe, the
fourteenth-century "morning star of the Reformation," put it this
way: "The holiest of all are the most tempted of all. The higher the
mountain, the greater the wind. God plays with his child the way
a mother sometimes hides from a little one. Soon enough, there
will be hugs and a wiping away of tears."

In 1991 Texas oil billionaire Edward Bass built Biosphere 2, a
hermetically sealed glass terrarium near Tucson, Arizona. Eight
scientists from seven countries lived in the dome in order to learn
whether humans could replicate Planet Earth's complex ecosys-
tem and thrive in an artificial environment. The glass dome seem-
ingly had everything common to earth's environment: oxygen,
insects, fish, simulated rain forest, soil for growing food, artificial

ocean replicated by a wave machine and so on. The scientists were encouraged when plants and trees in the atrium grew more quickly than others in the wild. But they were perplexed when many fell over before reaching reproductive age. After studying the problem scientists concluded that absence of wind in the terrarium produced trees with much weaker wood than similar species in the wild. Biosphere 2 illustrates the fact that strong headwinds are necessary to produce hardy species. The trials and suffering we experience in this life ultimately make our character and our souls stronger as we journey toward heaven.

EXTREME ASCETIC AFFLICTIONS

Recognizing the redemptive value of suffering but misguided about its place in our lives, some Christians have unwisely afflicted themselves. Severe asceticism (i.e., harsh treatment of the body) was practiced by some desert fathers who believed that the physical body weighed down the soul and so must be mortified. The desert father Antony of Egypt (c. 251-356) lived a life of severe asceticism, fasting in the Sinai wilderness for eighty-five years. Certain Egyptian monks were known as "sleepless ones" because they resisted sleep to engage in ceaseless prayer. Simeon the Stylite (c. 390-459) sat atop a sixty-foot pillar for thirty years, until his death. "The bones and sinews [were] visible on his feet due to the pain. Simeon loved his pain so much that he tortured himself to death."

Some monks practiced ascetic rigor by surviving on bread and water, sleeping on beds of nails, wearing coats of thorns, and treading barefoot on snakes and scorpions. Bernard of Clairvaux (1090-1153) practiced extended fasts and sleep deprivation that impaired his health. He wrote, "The flesh of God's revered servant, hardened and virtually mineralized by tough vigils and pared to the bones by pitiless dieting, would smell after death as 'sweet as a perfumed apple.' " The German mystic Henry Suso (c. 1300-1366) pounded a cross into his own back, persuaded that the pain inflicted would substitute for greater torments in the life to come. We must not think that God regards us more favorably because of self-afflicted punishment. Suffering inevitably affects all humans in their lifetime, but Scripture never advises us to inflict it on ourselves. The apostle Paul weighed in against "false humility" and "harsh treatment of the body" that "lack any value in restraining sensual indulgence" (Col 2:23). Jean Pierre de Caussade described souls who pursue paths of severe self-mortification as "extremely unmortified in their mortification." Spiritual disciplines performed in love facilitate Christlike maturity, but they neither remove sin nor bring favor with God. Since God alone knows what trials and afflictions will benefit us, we gladly allow him to choose our afflictions.

COMFORT AMIDST TRIALS

Like a rushing stream, human nature seeks the path of least resistance. Ours has been called a culture of "suffering avoidance" because our human tendency is usually to avoid whatever causes distress and pain (unlike the ascetics). God has not promised that Christians will be exempt from suffering. He *has* promised that we will never walk alone in our trials, and we indeed have a great high priest who understands and has experienced our afflictions (Heb 4:15). Through a distressing event, God may be calling us to engage unfinished spiritual and emotional business from an earlier stage of our journey. A trial may represent an invitation to surrender some cherished area of our life that we need to release to

"Peace on this earth consists in accepting the things that are contrary to our desires, not in being exempted from suffering them, nor in being delivered from all temptations."

FRANÇOIS FÉNELON

our Lord. Almost always it will involve the summons to commit more intentionally to kingdom priorities as Jesus' disciples.

Some see an inconsistency between troublesome trials and Jesus' invitation, "Take my yoke upon you and learn from me. . . . For my yoke is easy and my burden is light" (Mt 11:29-30). However, the yoke Jesus referred to is the burden of meticulous adherence to the law and the Pharisaic regulations. When weighed down with life's inevitable trials Jesus comes alongside, bears our burdens and binds up our wounds. However searing the fire, he quenches the flames with grace sufficient for the ordeal. Paul learned from personal experience that God's faithfulness never fails. "He will not let you be tempted beyond what you can bear. But when you are tempted, he will also provide a way out so that you can endure it" (1 Cor 10:13).

> *"I would not consider any spirituality worthwhile that wants to walk in sweetness and ease and run from the imitation of Christ."*
>
> JOHN OF THE CROSS

Jesus is our model when disorientation distresses our soul. Our Lord insisted that both he and his followers must tread the path of suffering. Faithful disciples can be expected to suffer as did Jesus, for "servants are not greater than their master" (Jn 15:20). This common apostolic theme teaches that just as Jesus was not spared suffering, neither will his friends. Francis of Assisi noted, "If this was God's way on earth, what choice have I but to make it my own?" Christians who endure distressing trials participate, as Peter observed, in the sufferings of our Lord himself (1 Pet 4:13). It often turns out that the greater our sufferings, the greater our fellowship with Christ becomes.

Perplexity and distress, then, constitute tools by which God refines us. Paul put it this way: "There's far more to this life than trusting in Christ. There's also suffering for him. And the suffering is as much a gift as the trusting" (Phil 1:29 *The Message*). Hardships, transformation and inheriting the kingdom are all closely connected. Through all life's unnerving trials God remains our provider, protector and ever-present friend.

Poet and hymn writer William Cowper (1731-1800) suffered periods of severe depression and eventually an emotional breakdown that led to commitment to a mental hospital. Cowper's poems and hymns, born of spiritual and emotional distress, encourage afflicted saints to persevere in the Lord and his ways. Ponder the following stanzas of Cowper's much-loved hymn "God Moves in a Mysterious Way" (1774).

> God moves in a mysterious way,
>   His wonders to perform;
> He plants his footsteps on the sea,
>   And rides upon the storm
>
> Judge not the Lord by feeble sense,
>   But trust him for his grace;
> Behind a frowning providence,
>   He hides a smiling face.

FOR INDIVIDUAL OR GROUP REFLECTION AND DISCUSSION

1. How has reading this chapter helped you better understand that God often uses suffering, however distressing, to advance your spiritual growth and love for him?

2. Recall a major season of spiritual or emotional imbalance in your life. How did you respond to its challenge? How difficult was it to trust God implicitly in the trial rather than seek a way of escape or perhaps rebel against him?

3. Review your life journey thus far. How has God used seasons of distress and disorientation to facilitate dying to self and to realize his purpose for your life?

3 *Painful Disorientation*

Understanding Why We Suffer

"I eat ashes as my food

and mingle my drink with tears. . . .

My days are like the evening shadow;

I wither away like grass."

PSALM 102:9, 11

A good friend, whom I will call Brian, has had a distinguished career serving several leading Christian organizations. Brian and his wife, Sarah, who met while working overseas, enjoyed a storybook marriage. Some years later, however, tragedy struck. Their son, a ski-patrol worker, lost his life in a skiing accident. Later their daughter succumbed to breast cancer after a long illness. As Brian phased into retirement, Sarah was presented with a diagnosis of early Alzheimer's disease. A CAT scan later showed, however, that this diagnosis was in error and that she suffered from hydro encephalitis, where the pressure on her brain was twenty times normal. Sarah quickly deteriorated before Brian's eyes and within weeks passed away.

Following his wife's death Brian felt trapped in loneliness, asking, *How will I live without my beloved Sarah? How could all this have happened to one who loves the Lord and has given his life to servicing others?* Moreover, Brian became angry with the medical community and even with God himself.

After his shock and grief subsided somewhat, Brian pondered the dreadful hand that he had been dealt. Were these painful, gut-wrenching calamities an inevitable consequence of the human condition? Or had he simply been the victim of medical misjudgment and neglect? Had his beloved family fallen prey to brutal attacks from the devil and his minions? Or did God permit these disasters in order to serve some higher purpose, such as bringing unsaved family and friends to Christ? As faith seeks understanding, can we also comprehend to some degree *why* saints such as Brian suffer so this side of heaven? In this chapter, with guidance from Scripture and saints of the past, we'll seek to understand the principal sources of the disorientation that we often experience on our faith journeys.

THE SINFUL HUMAN HEART

The most common cause of soul distress comes from remnants of the sinful nature still present in believers. Evil desires and passions that remain unchecked compromise the peace Christ gave to his people. We worsen the effects of our fallen nature with poor choices and destructive behaviors. Theologian and church leader Augustine of Hippo (354-430) correctly observed, "Think of the great variety of punishments which afflict the human race, not as the outcome of the malice and wickedness of evil men but simply as the native condition and common lot of human misery."

An internal struggle takes place between the Christian's old fleshly nature and God's indwelling Spirit. Sinful human desires and the Holy Spirit contend with one another in a lively struggle. As Paul put it: "For the sinful nature desires what is contrary to the Spirit, and the Spirit what is contrary to the sinful nature. They are in conflict with each other, so that you are not to do whatever you want" (Gal 5:17).

"So did my two wills, one new,

the other old, one spiritual,

the other carnal, fight within

me and by their discord

undo my soul."

AUGUSTINE OF HIPPO

Unconfessed sins drive a relational wedge between the soul and God. Isaiah reminded wayward Israel, "But your iniquities have separated / you from your God; your sins have hidden his face from you" (Is 59:2). Scripture states, for example, that those who fail to love brothers and sisters in Christ walk in darkness (1 Jn 2:11). When fellowship with God is strained, the believing soul becomes distressed. As David sorrowfully wrote, "When you hid your face, I was dismayed" (Ps 30:7).

Moreover, problems such as pride, resentment, anger and compulsive behavior patterns compromise communion with God. Ungodly impulses and actions consign the soul to a gray world, where God appears distant. Unconfessed sins blunt our prayer experience, resulting in spiritual unease. As the psalmist put it, "If I had cherished sin in my heart, / the Lord would not have listened" (Ps 66:18). Francis of Sales observed, "Tiny sins will not kill your soul, but if they wrap a tangle of bad habits around you, devotion will suffer."

The conscience is the moral evaluator of the heart; therefore sin breeds a troubling sense of guilt in us. Following his sins of adultery and murder David lamented, "My guilt has overwhelmed me / like a burden too heavy to bear" (Ps 38:4). The prophet Isaiah proclaimed a timeless moral truism:

> But the wicked are like the tossing sea,
>> which cannot rest,
>> whose waves cast up mire and mud.
> "There is no peace," says my God, "for the wicked."
> (Is 57:20-21)

The Welsh Presbyterian Christopher Love declared, "If you break God's law, God will break your peace," adding, "Concealed guilt may not bring a child of God to hell, yet for a time it may bring a hell into his conscience."

Since a human is a unity of soul and body, unconfessed sins manifest themselves symptomatically in emotional and physical distress. Reflecting on his adultery with Bathsheba and scheming to murder her husband Uriah, David again gave voice to his torment:

> When I kept it all inside,
>> my bones turned to powder,
>> my words became daylong groans.
> The pressure never let up;
>> all the juices of my life dried up. (Ps 32:3-4 *The Message*)

Unconfessed sin grieves the Father and invites his loving discipline. Moses warned the Israelites that if they failed to obey the Lord, distressing calamities would overtake them. The psalmist testified, "The LORD has chastened me severely, / but he has not given me over to death" (Ps 118:18). The writer to the Hebrews taught that God disciplines his children much as a loving parent disciplines his or her child (Heb 12:5-11). We are better off to heed his discipline and come forward with our faults than to continue on the dangerous road of blatant sin.

A major source of the Christian's anguish, then, is unresolved sin. The fallen human heart could be described as the hardware of sin—the root cause of many of our distresses. How important, then, for us as Christians to keep short accounts with God by

"The worst enemies we have

are lodged in our own heart and

in our very flesh and blood.

They wake, sleep, and live with

us, as an evil guest whom we

have invited into our house and

now cannot get rid of."

MARTIN LUTHER

examining conscience and correcting all known wrongs.

THE FALLEN WORLD ORDER

The New Testament employs two main Greek words for world. Our interest here is with the word *kosmos*, which refers to the world order operating on principles hostile to God and his people. The *kosmos* is a dark system—a toxic environment characterized by corruption and decay. As expressed by the apostle John, "The whole world *[kosmos]* is under the control of the evil one" (1 Jn 5:19).

God calls us as disciples of Jesus to transform the world. Our task in this world is to be fruitfully involved in working with God as he builds his kingdom. But given our identification with Christ we do not belong to the *kosmos* (Jn 15:19). In the sixteenth century John Calvin observed that because we are citizens of another world we often are "stripped of our possessions," "reduced to penury," "cast out of our own house," "vexed and despised," "branded with disgrace and ignominy," and even "slain." Things have not changed much through the centuries. Although we may be reluctant to admit it, the unbelieving world despises Christians even as it despised Jesus during his life on earth. Hostile opposition from enemies of the cross has been the lot of God's people throughout the centuries. Some believers may become so browbeaten by maltreatment and persecution as to abandon faith and forsake Christ.

While serving in this world Christians are susceptible to the allure of its attractions—by enticements presented to the senses. Believers unwittingly may conform to the pattern of the world or be squeezed into the mold of its cravings and values. If careless and undiscerning, we may become tainted and even controlled by the fallen moral and spiritual environment. As God's people we may set our hearts on this present world order, as did Demas who abandoned discipleship because "he loved this world" (2 Tim 4:10). Saints may be overcome with worldliness, the essence of which is uncritically setting our hearts on the values of the culture without regard for the instruction of God's Word.

If we allow ourselves to be captivated by the world with its deep-rooted evil, we put ourselves in spiritual danger. Bonding with the world distances our souls from God, resulting in poverty of spirit. As John plainly put it, "If you love the world, love for the Father is not in you" (1 Jn 2:15). If we who belong to another and better world allow ourselves to be enticed by this world, we will have conflicted hearts. Such divided affection leads to sorrow in our souls.

> *"The whole world is in crisis.*
> *A kind of madness sweeps*
> *through human society,*
> *threatening to destroy it*
> *altogether."*
>
> THOMAS MERTON

SATAN AND DEMONS

Not all distress and suffering is due to sin or the broken world order. The Gospel account of the man born blind (Jn 9:1-12) establishes this truism and shows that many of our troubles are brought about directly by the seductions of the devil.

Scripture assigns names to Satan that highlight his deceptive and destructive activity:

- enemy (Mt 13:25, 39)

- evil one (Mt 13:19)

- prince of demons (Mk 3:22)

- father of lies (Jn 8:44)

- murderer (Jn 8:44)

- god of this age (2 Cor 4:4)

- angel of light (2 Cor 11:14)

- tempter (1 Thess 3:5)

- roaring lion (1 Pet 5:8)

The chief of fallen angels roams the earth, seeking to outwit saints with his seductive schemes. In the words of Peter, "The Devil is poised to pounce, and would like nothing better than to catch you napping" (1 Pet 5:8 *The Message*). The evil one presents himself as an angel of light, constantly trying to deceive God's people. Satan's chief aim is to deflect hearts from the worship and service of the true God. Paul acknowledged that "our struggle is not against flesh and blood, but against the rulers, against the authorities, against the powers of this dark world and against the spiritual forces of evil in the heavenly realms" (Eph 6:12).

"Satan attempts to subvert us both by delight in wickedness and by hidden snares, fraudulently passing off evil things for good with the most subtle finesse."

JOHN CASSIAN

Our spiritual foe knows well our areas of weakness and vulnerability. When we let down our guard, the devil and his minions move in for the kill. Satan skillfully directs his attacks at our weakest point. As the Puritan preacher Richard Sibbes (1537-1635) notes, "It is Satan's practice to go over the hedge where it is lowest." The evil one preys on Christians' sinful nature to afflict the soul and create discouragement—perhaps even despair. If the human heart can be represented as the hardware of sin, the world's enticements and Satan's assaults constitute the software.

The devil distresses believing hearts in several significant ways.

In the first place, he attacks our minds, aiming to deceive us. He undermines God's truth and fills our minds with lies, thus weakening our faith. The evil one engenders false images of God, suggesting that God is uncaring toward his children or—worse yet— that he is a ruthless tyrant intent on doing us in. False depictions of God distress the soul and impede our relationship with him.

Satan also appeals to our sinful nature by leading us to believe that the pleasures of sin are worth our indulging. Many saints are deceived by this angel of light. Moreover, Satan arouses disturbing passions such as fear, anger, lust and depression. Unholy impulses agitate the soul, destroying our peace. We see this tormenting work in the experience of Saul in the Old Testament. The Spirit of God departed from him, opening the door to torment from an evil spirit (1 Sam 16:14)—a spirit that drove him to insanity. Satan subtly assaults areas of personal woundedness such as low self-worth and the need for approval. He deepens compulsive behavior patterns like workaholism and perfectionism.

The tempter provokes us to commit blatant sins (sins of commission) and to fail to do the good things that honor God (sins of omission). If the evil one sorely tempted the Son of God, how much more can he bewitch one of us to sin? There are numerous biblical examples of Satan's solicitations to sin. He provoked, for example, David to take a census of Israel, and he incited Judas to betray Jesus. Satan goaded Ananias to lie to God and selfishly keep part of the proceeds of property that he and his wife had sold.

Satan, furthermore, attacks our consciences with false guilt and shame. The accuser causes us to be "overwhelmed by excessive sorrow" (2 Cor 2:7)—at times to the point of despair. Through such activity we lose the sense of God's comforting presence. The evil one, in addition, assails overly scrupulous consciences with negative messages such as, "Those who struggle with a persistent sin have fallen from grace and forfeited heaven," or "Your actions prove that you never were a Christian in the first place." A Puritan pastor astutely observed, "Because [Satan] cannot keep you from having grace, he will keep you as long as he can from having the sense of grace."

Satan can also cause physical afflictions. The book of Job recounts that "Satan went out from the presence of the LORD and afflicted Job with painful sores from the soles of his feet to the crown of his head" (Job 2:7). So extensive were Job's physical afflictions that his wife urged him to curse God and die. Satan also caused a Jewish woman to be bound by a crippling paralysis for eighteen years (Lk 13:11, 16). The apostle Paul testified that his thorn in the flesh, or distressing physical illness, was "a messenger of Satan" (2 Cor 12:7). There's no doubt that our physical and mental misfortunes may be brought on by evil spiritual powers.

Satan incites persecution against Jesus' followers. While teaching the disciples on the Mount of Olives our Lord predicted this would be the case in the present age: "You will be handed over to be persecuted and put to death, and you will be hated by all nations because of me" (Mt 24:9). To the church at Smyrna John wrote, "the devil will put some of you in prison to test you, and you will suffer persecution for ten days" (Rev 2:10). Satanic oppression against God's people continues unabated in a world supposedly informed by principles of compassion and human rights.

When teaching a few years ago in an ecumenical setting, I mentioned in passing Satan and his seductive activity. After the session a female minister from a mainline denomination chided me, saying, "You don't believe in a literal devil do you?" I replied that I do believe in the devil, having read about him in Scripture and having met him in personal experience. A day or so later a liturgy of welcoming the Holy Spirit was conducted in which the celebrant invited those who did not personally know the Spirit of God to come forward for prayer. The woman who had taken me to task stepped out, visibly shaken, to receive the Spirit into her life. In a social time that followed, the woman hugged me and said, "I guess I'll have to change my theology too."

In our own strength we are helpless to fight against the dark spiritual powers. To successfully withstand the evil one we must clothe ourselves with the full armor of God, remaining constant in prayer and ever vigilant. Then, "yell a loud no to the Devil and watch him scamper. Say a quiet yes to God and he'll be there in no time" (Jas 4:7-8 *The Message*). The good news is that Satan may darken the lamp within believing hearts, but he can never extinguish it.

LIFE'S DISTRESSING MISFORTUNES

Some of our problems might also be caused by an external crisis, such as a career failure, death of a loved one, economic dislocations or natural disasters. As I write, tens of thousands of people have died from an earthquake in central China measuring 7.9 on the Richter scale. Furthermore, a hundred thousand people have died from a cyclone that hit impoverished Myanmar (Burma), with warnings that a million more may succumb from starvation and disease. Both non-Christians and Christians who survive major disasters suffer grievously.

Our troubles might be due to an internal distress, such as a physical affliction or an emotional illness. The human body and mind are so incredibly complex that any one of a multitude of systems can malfunction and bring about great suffering.

> "God makes use of the inconstancy, the ingratitude of men, the disappointments, the failures which attend human prosperity, to detach us from the created world and its good things."
>
> FRANÇOIS FÉNELON

We may be troubled by major physical maladies such as heart disease, cancer or dementia. A Christian may also deal with psychological burnout, a depressive episode or other emotional illness.

External and internal stressors often trouble our souls. While life at times seems calm and secure, it can quickly become destabilized and unglued. As I have noted, God has not promised his children exemption from suffering; he has, however, pledged to be with us and comfort us in our trials. In his wisdom God uses life's painful misfortunes to drain us of self-sufficiency and lead us to trust and depend on him. In the mystery of providence, our difficult trials offer opportunities for healing, transformation and empowerment for service. Pain leads us to seek God and his purpose for our lives with greater intention.

A TRAUMATIC LIFE TRANSITION

The effects of a difficult life transition may also lead to distressing disorientation. The transition from childhood to adolescence often is disruptive, as any parent of a teenage child can attest. However, my focus here is limited to adults at midlife. Dissatisfaction with life, marriage, career path or relationship with God can strain our emotional and spiritual resources. The so-called midlife crisis is said to occur anywhere between ages thirty-five and fifty-five. Not every person experiences a distressing midlife transition, but should it occur it may last for months or even years.

The midlife transition distresses at several levels. Midlifers face a crisis of identity and are filled with self-doubt. They typically ask, Who am I? and Who do I want to become? Western culture's preference for youth over maturity may contribute to a sense of worthlessness. With the peak of personal accomplishments past, midlifers may feel that they are on a treadmill going nowhere. Filled with anxiety, they may ask, Is this all there is to life? As midlifers sense that their best years are behind them, they experience the first full flush of anxiety at the threatening prospect of their own mortality.

Emotionally, unhealthy life patterns practiced for so many

years can lead to anxiety, irritability, fatigue and apathy—possibly even loss of interest in life itself. Classical Christian authorities called this kind of spiritual apathy *acedia*, symptoms of which include spiritual listlessness, slackened attention, sadness and boredom. We see evidence of acedia in the experience of Elijah languishing under the juniper tree (1 Kings 19:4-5).

Physically, a difficult midlife transition may manifest itself in bodily distress. The aging body loses vigor and slows down, and midlifers may be distressed by the gradual deterioration of their outward appearance. Second-half folks become more easily fatigued by the pressure and stress of long hours on the job. At midlife the daily routine may become a tedious and unfulfilling grind. Midlife people are "simply tired of having a tired body."

Midlifers may also become stressed relationally and socially. After two decades or so, a marriage may become monotonous, or the years of preoccupation with career advancement may have resulted in relational neglect. One partner may seek to recapture the excitement of romance through an extramarital affair, either emotional or physical. The trauma of divorce threatens insecure marriages in the midlife zone.

Midlifers may also experience career dissatisfaction. They may hate their work but can't afford to quit. As attractive employment opportunities elsewhere shrink, workers become increasingly anxious at the realization that time is running out. Ambitious goals established earlier now seem unachievable. "The successful person is confronted with the aching 'So what?' and the unsuccessful person with 'I'll never make it now!' "

If we've failed to give attention to our spiritual growth in the earlier part of life, at midlife we may find ourselves strangely disinterested in the things of God. More perplexing still, we may find ourselves in a distressing dark night of the soul, concluding that God is not real or that he has failed to show up when we need him most. Confronted with the painful absence of spiritual comforts, we may be tempted to abandon faith and turn to other religious or philosophical alternatives as potential sources of satisfaction.

At midlife "we move from knowing who we think we are to not knowing who we are at all." The stress accumulates and the soul threatens to implode. Midlifers need to see the opportunity for growth afforded by the distresses rather than flee from their challenges. The midlife transition represents an invitation to launch an intentional inner journey with the potential for radical transformation. Midlifers need to face up to the reality that "we cannot live the afternoon of life according to the program of life's morning."

THE SPIRIT OF GOD

Since God is ultimately in control of the universe, we might say that he somehow mysteriously ordains our circumstances. Puritan pastors and theologians delighted to point out that "all God's dealings with his people are in a way of grace, including his visitations of trouble." Hardships and afflictions, however, prove to be evidence not of God's wrath but of his love. God's ways, though mysterious to us, are neither wrong nor sinful, for he is the Holy One. The Bible provides ample evidence that in some circumstances God's Spirit is behind our distresses.

Job considered God the ultimate source of his troubles, though he used the agency of Satan to accomplish his aims. Job testified about the Almighty:

> He has shrouded my paths in darkness.
> He has stripped me of my honor
>   and removed the crown from my head.
> He tears me down on every side till I am gone;
>   he uproots my hope like a tree. (Job 19:8-10)

Job further lamented:

> He would crush me with a storm
>   and multiply my wounds for no reason.

> He would not let me catch my breath
> but would overwhelm me with misery. (Job 9:17-18)

In dialogue with God David reflected, "I will keep quiet, I will not say a word, for you are the one who made me suffer like this" (Ps 39:9 TEV). David understood that God brought trials into his life in order to lead him to repentance and ultimately to wholeness. The sons of Korah in Psalm 44:9-14 cried out to God for the reproach and disgrace they suffered through defeat in battle. They proclaimed: "You gave us up to be devoured like sheep" (Ps 44:11).

Other biblical people attributed their distressing circumstances to God's mysterious initiative in their lives:

- Isaiah testified that God creates both "darkness" and "disaster" (Is 45:7). The prophet announced to the wayward people of Israel that God bestows "the bread of adversity and the water of affliction" (Is 30:20).

- Hosea, speaking of God, wrote:

> He has torn us to pieces
> but he will heal us;
> he has injured us
> but he will bind up our wounds. (Hos 6:1)

- Jeremiah lamented God's judgment on Israel as punishment for sins.

> Is any suffering like my suffering . . .
> that the LORD brought on me
> in the day of his fierce anger?
> From on high he sent fire,
> sent it down into my bones.
> He spread a net for my feet
> and turned me back.
> He made me desolate,
> faint all the day long. (Lam 1:12-13)

The weeping prophet announced that God had planned and executed Israel's calamities. Nevertheless, God's love and faithfulness toward his wayward people remained constant and unfailing.

• Jesus in John 15 painted the picture of a gardener who clips and prunes living branches of a vine so they can bear more abundant fruit. The Father is the vinedresser who tends the vine with a knife; Jesus is the vine and believers are the branches grafted into the vine. God's loving pruning action often causes distress, but also facilitates growth. Commentating on this imagery, Martin Luther noted that the Christian's affliction "is God's way of fertilizing him."

• The writer of Hebrews insisted that God disciplines his people for their eternal welfare (Heb 12:6-11). In order to form his children into the image of his beloved Son, God skillfully cuts away at the old sinful nature.

Many reliable and trusted Christian authorities have taught that at times God orchestrates seasons of ambiguity and distress in the lives of his people for their eternal welfare:

• Van Ruysbroeck (1293-1381), the Flemish spiritual writer, made the point very simply: God "has sometimes sent us sickness for our own good."

• Thomas à Kempis (c. 1380-1471) imagined God addressing believers with these reassuring words: "Do not consider yourself forsaken if I send some temporary hardship or withdraw the comforts you desire. For this is the way to the kingdom of heaven."

• François Fénelon (1651-1715) declared, "God is a clever designer of crosses. Some are as heavy as iron or lead. Others are as light as straw. . . . In spite of their great variety, crosses have two things in common. They are hard to carry and they crucify."

Scripture and these Christian authorities confirm that dis-

tresses of soul and body are not always due to human fault or
failure. After being defeated by a godless enemy, inspired Hebrew
songwriters lamented:

> All this came upon us,
>> though we had not forgotten you;
>> we had not been false to your covenant.
> Our hearts had not turned back;
>> our feet had not strayed from your path.
> But you crushed us and made us a haunt for jackals;
> you covered us over with deep darkness. (Ps 44:17-19)

Since we believers are united by faith with Christ, God is always with us. Yet in the mystery of his providence, sometimes we
cannot feel God's presence. The psalmist affirmed,

> LORD, when you favored me,
>> you made my royal mountain stand firm;
> but when you hid your face,
>> I was dismayed. (Ps 30:7)

Christians have called this perceived absence of God's comforts
"the dark night of the soul." The phrase is used more loosely now
(especially in pop spirituality), but only God's intentional withdrawal of spiritual comforts, in order
to conform us to Christ, constitutes
the classical dark night of the soul.

"Whoever brings an affliction, it is God that sends it."

THOMAS WATSON

While I addressed these issues
with an adult education class, a fifty-
something gentleman suddenly stood
up and shouted with a loud voice, "Why has no one told me this
before? I have been involved in a Bible-believing church for thirty
years; but I have never been informed of the possibility that my
soul's desolation may be caused not by sin but by the Spirit's providential work in my life." He then added, "This morning the bur-

den I have been carrying for years has been lifted from my shoulders!" On another occasion a Baptist pastor responded, "For the first time in my life I understand what is going on in the dark places of my inner world." We'll explore more fully the phenomenon of the dark night of the soul in chapter four.

REDEMPTIVE SEASONS

Through all our hardships and sufferings the Father works to refine and mature us. We may be tempted to conclude from our trials that God is angry with us, but God loves us deeply and is pleased with us, his children clothed with the righteousness of his Son. By means of our sufferings the all-wise Father works on our hearts and renews our lives. Through our struggles and trials he removes the illusion of self-sufficiency and woos us into a posture of surrender. We cannot dismiss the considerable emphasis on suffering in the Bible—not least in Peter's first letter. God knows that for his people to be transformed we need darkness as well as light, adversity as well as prosperity, and—yes—bad times as well as good times. The following striking statement of Martin Luther is not a total exaggeration: "When God wants to build people up, He first tears them down. When God wants to heal, He first breaks in pieces. Whom God wants to bring to life, He first kills."

"Strict as God seems to be in his dealings with us, he never inflicts any sufferings solely to give pain. He always has the purification of the soul in view. The severity of the operation is caused by the depth of the malady to be cured."

FRANÇOIS FÉNELON

Painful affliction is God's "strange work," his "alien task" (Is 28:21), as Luther loved to point out. In his famous manual of Christian doctrine, *Institutes of the Christian Religion*, John Calvin explained at length God's sometimes painful education of his children. "In the very harshness of tribulations we must recognize the kindness and generosity of our Father toward us, since he does not even then cease to promote our salvation. For he afflicts us not to ruin or destroy us but, rather, to free us from the condemnation of the world."

Most schools of secular psychology view distress and pain as problems to be solved or at least relieved. Christian formation, however, sees God's loving hand refining our character and drawing us into deeper intimacy with himself through our experience of pain. Distress and suffering thus occupy a prominent place in God's redemptive economy.

The compassionate Father perfectly knows our struggles and afflictions, and we can be confident that he is with us in our trials, even if our sense of his presence occasionally burns dim. Jesus not only is with us in our trials, but as our great high priest he actually enters into our afflictions. The greater we suffer the greater his compassionate heart showers us with mercy and goodness.

In his timing God will make the bitter waters of suffering sweet, and we will one day exchange the cross we bear for a crown. Since God always works for our eternal welfare, we shouldn't give in to discouragement or despondency in difficult times. Rather, we must cling firmly to the faithful and merciful Lord, even while pouring out our hearts to him with sighs and tears. May our response to life's distressing circumstances be that of Job, who suffered unimaginable loss:

> Blessed are those whom God corrects; . . .
> For he wounds, but he also binds up;
>   he injures, but his hands also heal. (Job 5:17-18)

FOR INDIVIDUAL OR GROUP REFLECTION AND DISCUSSION

1. Which of the spiritual factors cited in this chapter appear to be

the greatest source of your present challenges and struggles? Give specific examples from life experiences on your journey.

2. What do you sense to be the chief area of weakness and vulnerability in your life that Satan exploits to hinder your maturation in Christ and fruitfulness in kingdom service? Give some leading examples.

3. Prayerfully ponder the extent and manner in which you feel that the loving God mysteriously may be behind your trials and afflictions. How have you felt in these circumstances?

4 Painful Disorientation

Dark Night of the Soul

"My God, my God, why have you forsaken me?

Why are you so far from saving me? . . .

My God, I cry out by day, but you do not answer,

by night, but I find no rest."

PSALM 22:1-2

After several years of ministry a young associate pastor found himself in what he described as a black hole. Pastor Don shared with a close friend, "I have a degree in theology, read the Bible and pray regularly. But for several months I've experienced a spirit of confusion and desolation that has eroded my faith in God and the church. Recently I confessed to my senior pastor that I don't believe much of anything anymore. It's devastating to be in the position of trying to help others while being unable to help myself."

As described by classical Christian authorities, the dark night
of the soul represents a specific form of painful disorientation
characterized by the perceived absence of God's comforting presence and lack of satisfaction in spiri-
tual pursuits. Some Christians overlook the phenomenon of the dark
night because they believe God
would never withdraw his presence
and spiritual comforts from his chil-
dren. We are often reluctant to talk about spiritual dryness, fearing that others will think we're unspiritual.

*"During the night we must
wait for the light."*

FRANCIS OF SALES

Church historian Martin Marty entered a dark time following
the death of his wife, Elsa, from cancer. His moving story is recorded in his book *A Cry of Absence: Reflections on the Winter of the
Heart*. Processing his personal pain through the gut-wrenching
experiences of ancient psalmists, Marty spoke of dark places, divine distance, spiritual abandonment and the sense of dying spiritually. Well-meaning friends asked, "Why should anyone be abandoned to illness or spiritual agony unless she deserved it? God is
good, so suffering has to be punishment." Disoriented by his loss,
Marty lamented, "Why, O God, after a remission of disease, is it
allowed to come back relentlessly until malignant cells kill? . . .
Why, O Hidden One . . . Why, O Silence . . . Why, O Absence,
when the cry is most intense is the silence most stunning? The
passionate heart searches for answers."

WELL-DOCUMENTED IN SCRIPTURE

The theme of darkness occurs frequently in the Bible. The first
chapter of Genesis describes the physical darkness that enveloped
the newly created cosmos. In the spiritual realm one of the figurative meanings of darkness is the sense of confusion and desolation
resulting from God's hiddenness. The Old Testament records numerous instances of biblical figures who struggled with darkness

due to God's perceived absence from their experience.

Job experienced a long period of painful darkness—the word appearing some thirty times in the book bearing his name. Job surely was a virtuous man: "blameless and upright; he feared God and shunned evil" (Job 1:1). Nevertheless, stripped of his children, possessions and health, Job concluded that God had abandoned him. Job lamented,

> *"Why do you hide your face*
>
> *and consider me your enemy?"*
>
> JOB 13:24

God "has blocked my way so I cannot pass; / he has shrouded my paths in darkness" (Job 19:8). Feel Job's pain as he raised his fist heavenward:

> Night pierces my bones; . . .
> I cry out to you, God, but you do not answer; . . .
> When I hoped for good, evil came;
>   when I looked for light, then came darkness.
> (Job 30:17, 20, 26)

Nevertheless, Job never lost all hope in God, as reflected in his magnificent confession later in the book.

Psalmists poured out their feelings of abandonment in inspired songs. "Why, LORD, do you stand far off? / Why do you hide yourself in times of trouble?" (Ps 10:1). Longingly, David cried out, "How long, LORD? Will you forget me forever? / How long will you hide your face from me?" (Ps 13:1). Psalm 22 rehearses David's experience of divine desertion that anticipates the desolation of Christ on the cross. In another song David attributed his melancholic spirit to God apparently having forgotten him (Ps 42:9-10).

Asaph the psalmist also experienced painful abandonment, prompting his anguished questioning:

> Will the Lord reject forever?
>   Will he never show his favor again?
> Has his unfailing love vanished forever? (Ps 77:7-8)

The sons of Korah stated their opinion that God brought darkness on them:

> All this came upon us,
>   though we had not forgotten you;
>   we had not been false to your covenant.
> Our hearts had not turned back;
>   our feet had not strayed from your path.
> But you crushed us and made us a haunt for jackals;
>   you covered us with deep darkness. (Ps 44:17-19)

Yet another psalm laments the singer's darkness of soul. "You have put me in the lowest pit, / in the darkest depths" (Ps 88:6). The psalm continues: "Why, LORD, do you reject me / and hide your face from me? . . . You have taken from me friend and neighbor— / darkness is my closest friend" (Ps 88:14, 18).

Other people in the Old Testament experienced the distressing darkness of a spiritual night:

- The Hebrews in Egyptian slavery. For 430 years God's oppressed people struggled with the silence of God. Where was the covenant God of Abraham, Isaac and Jacob? Why had God been distant all those years? Even Moses questioned God's failure to deliver his people. "Ever since I went to Pharaoh to speak in your name, he has brought trouble on this people, and you have not rescued your people at all" (Ex 5:23).

- Israel in foreign captivity. During seven decades of foreign captivity, God's covenant people walked in darkness (Is 50:10). God explained, "For a brief moment I abandoned you. . . . / In a surge of anger / I hid my face from you" (Is 54:7-8). Jeremiah lamented:

> He has driven me away
>   and made me walk in darkness rather than light; . . .
> He has made me dwell in darkness
>   like those long dead. (Lam 3:2, 6)

We can see the entire book of Lamentations as one painful and disorienting dark night both for the "weeping prophet" and for exiled Israel.

- Jonah. The prophet entered the place of deep darkness when a great fish entombed him for three days. When Jonah delivered God's message to Nineveh the people repented and God withheld his judgment, causing Jonah anger and frustration. The prophet entered yet another dark night in which he twice pled for God to allow him to die. "Now, LORD, take away my life, for it is better for me to die than to live" (Jon 4:3).

The New Testament also offers several examples of people who experienced spiritual darkness:

- Jesus. Our Lord himself experienced painful gloom in his final days on earth. After his arrest, Jesus' twelve friends—who earlier swore their unswerving allegiance—abandoned him. Deep darkness resulted when nailed to the Roman cross, stripped of his clothes and mocked, Jesus took upon himself the world's guilt. While suspended between heaven and earth—in the mystery of the atonement—the Father turned his back on his own Son. With fellowship between the Father and the Son momentarily broken, Jesus uttered his cry of dereliction—"My God, my God, why have you forsaken me?" (Mt 27:46). On the darkest of all dark nights—for a moment—God the Father deserted God the Son!

> *"The absence of God was a common experience in the company of the saved."*
>
> EUGENE PETERSON

- Mary and Martha. The sisters experienced anguish at Jesus' absence when their brother, Lazarus, died from a serious illness. When Lazarus was stricken the sisters sent word to Jesus to join them in this time of dire need, but Jesus remained where he was. After Lazarus had been in the tomb for four days, Jesus joined his friends and miraculously restored him to life (Jn 11:43-44).

- Mary the mother Jesus. Mary may have suffered a dark night of grief as she witnessed her beloved son nailed to the cross, shamefully humiliated and breathing his last (see Jn 19:25-27).

EXPERIENCED BY PROMINENT CHRISTIANS

Christians throughout history have suffered distressing darkness and offer us wisdom on how to deal with such circumstances. Consider the journeys of the following men and women of God.

In his native Spain, John of the Cross (1542-1591) pursued renewal, which was begun by Teresa of Ávila, of the Carmelite order. In 1577 friars opposed to John's reforms abducted him at night and led him blindfolded to the Carmelite monastery at Toledo. There they locked him for nine months in a small, windowless cell, flogged his bare back and provided only bread and water. Amidst the isolation and beatings of that dark place, John mentally composed his famous poems before escaping to safe havens where he wrote his longer prose works, including *The Dark Night of the Soul*. Physically frail, John traveled across Spain on a donkey teaching the transformational life Christ offers. He spent the last months of his life once again in solitary confinement, where he suffered ill health and died at age forty-nine.

C. S. Lewis (1893-1963) experienced a distressing dark night following the untimely death of his wife, Joy. When they were joined in marriage Joy suffered from bone cancer, but her condition dramatically improved, they believed, as a result of prayer. Less than a year later, however, Joy died—a victim of the cancer they thought had been cured. As a result of what Lewis described as "mad midnight moments"—where heaven seemed shut and God silent—the quintessential Christian apologist was overcome with despair, attributing his wife's terminal illness directly to

God. "Already, month by month and week by week you broke her body on the wheel whilst she still wore it. Is it not yet enough?" The penetrating insights into suffering Lewis had previously provided in *The Problem of Pain* (1940) no longer made sense to him. Overcome with grief, Lewis judged that God had abandoned him. Frustrated and angry, he called God a "Cosmic Sadist," reveling in "unreasonableness, vanity, vindictiveness, injustice, cruelty." For a time Lewis doubted almost everything he had ever believed about God. "Why is He so present a commander in our time of prosperity and so very absent a help in time of trouble?" Then one morning Lewis awoke to find that his anger and grief had vanished. Later he described his experience as "the painful silence of God." In his book *A Grief Observed*, Lewis showed how even stalwart believers can lose all sense of meaning in the universe and gradually learn to trust God again.

Mother Teresa of Calcutta (1910-1997) labored for nearly fifty years among the destitute and dying on the streets of Calcutta and beyond. For most of this time and until her death she testified to being in a dark night of the soul, experienced as "profound interior suffering, lack of sensible consolation, spiritual dryness, an apparent absence of God from her life, and, at the same time, a painful longing for Him." Mother Teresa believed that in God's secret providence darkness was purifying her imperfections, deepening her love for Jesus and intensifying her compassion for the poor. Sensing the importance of spiritual darkness to her vocation, Mother Teresa was content to live and serve in the distress of her dark night. She believed that by doing so she might become the light of Jesus to the unwanted and unloved, suffering in the darkness of unbelief. Teresa related to coworkers that the dark night allowed her in some measure to enter into the mystery of Christ's suffering on the cross. She wrote, "I have come to love the darkness, for I believe now that it is a part of a very, very small part of Jesus' darkness and pain on earth."

Thérèse of Lisieux (1873-1897), renowned for her "little Way" of suffering in love, endured a nightmare of pain physically from tuberculosis and spiritually from a year-and-a-half dark night in which she felt trapped in a pitch-black tunnel. In the darkness Thérèse felt that God had abandoned her and that heaven was uncertain. Duly exercised by the darkness, Thérèse learned to walk by faith and trust God whatever her circumstances.

Oswald Chambers (1874-1917), a Scottish-born Bible teacher, entered into a wilderness season in which spiritual loneliness obstructed the light of God's presence. In his popular devotional guide, *My Utmost for His Highest,* Chambers wrote the following concerning his dark night:

> After we have been perfectly related to God in sanctification, our faith has to be worked out in actualities. We shall be scattered, not into work, but into inner desolation and made to know what internal death to God's blessings means. . . . It is not that we choose it, but that God engineers our circumstances so that we are brought there. Until we have been through that experience, our faith is bolstered up by feelings and by blessings. . . . Darkness comes by the sovereignty of God. Are we prepared to let God do as He likes with us— prepared to be separated from conscious blessings?

Lewis Smedes (1922-2003), pastor and seminary professor, concluded from his dark night that God had abandoned him. He lamented, "I fell into a depression that made my family's life a misery, turned me into a grouch with my colleagues, made a hash of my relationship with God and pushed me into a dark night of the soul." For this difficult season Smedes leaned on the faith of his wife, Doris, and mustered the strength to *wait,* clinging desperately to God's promises. He later wrote, "God came back to me on the strength of her power to wait for me. Never before had I known the saving power of waiting."

Henri Nouwen (1932-1996), following the thirtieth anniversary of his ordination, experienced both depression and a dark night of the soul. He wrote, "Here I was . . . flat on the ground and in total darkness. What had happened? I had come face to face with my own nothingness. It was as if all that had given my life meaning was pulled away and I could see nothing in front of me but a bottomless abyss. . . . I felt that God had abandoned me." Fearing he might inflict harm on others, Nouwen left the L'Arche community to work on the loss of faith, sexual struggle and sense of abandonment that had immersed him in emotional and spiritual turmoil. Nouwen experienced light and healing by meditating on Jesus' parable of the prodigal son and Rembrandt's painting thereof displayed in the Hermitage in St. Petersburg, Russia.

EXPLAINED BY JOHN OF THE CROSS

No writer has explored the phenomenon of the dark night as thoroughly as John of the Cross (1542-1591), author of *The Ascent of Mount Carmel, The Dark Night, The Spiritual Canticle* and *The Living Flame of Love*. He saw the dark night as a necessary stage in our purifying ascent to loving union with God. We begin the journey, he claimed, as spiritual infants weaned on mother's milk, but to advance to spiritual maturity we must be stripped of earthly attachments through two dark nights. John called this phenomenon a *night* to distinguish it from the Christian's normal condition of spiritual sight. He called it *dark* to underscore the temporary withdrawal of God's illuminating presence.

John described two phases of the dark night, the first related to our senses (sight, hearing, touch, imagination, taste, smell) and the second to our spiritual nature (intellect, memory, will). John's two dark nights are not strictly sequential but overlap and interact with one another.

Immature Christians need the dark night of the senses to fight against fleshly desires. Given that we are naturally inclined to seek gratification in fleeting things, the dark night of the senses can help break us of destructive habits that hinder our love for God. In the darkness of the sensory night the mind fails to comprehend God as in former times, and satisfaction in prayer and other spiritual exercises diminishes. The senses must be purified both for the proper enjoyment of spiritual realities and to glorify God.

"God leaves them in such dryness that they not only fail to receive satisfaction and pleasure from their spiritual exercises and works as they formerly did, but also find these exercises distasteful and bitter."

JOHN OF THE CROSS

John envisioned two aspects of the dark night of the senses. In the *active* night we point ourselves toward God by surrendering the fleshly self and avoiding sins such as selfishness, pride and anger. We put aside anything that hinders our relationship with him and tame sinful desires and appetites by practicing spiritual disciplines like prayer and biblical meditation. Above all, we advance on the journey by pondering the life of Jesus and imitating his character and actions.

The *passive* night of the senses involves God's purifying action, depriving the soul of comforts that cause spiritual complacency. "In the passive night of the senses God is freeing us from the idols we have made of possessions, relationships, feelings, and behaviors." In this stage we might lose pleasure in spiritual exercises, particularly verbal prayer and meditation. Spiritual practices that were once life-giving become tedious. Through the passive night God burns away the sins that bind us to the past by the fire of his love.

The dark night of the senses typically is followed by a peaceful period that restores energies. "In this new state . . . [the soul] goes about the things of God with much more freedom and satisfaction of spirit and with more abundant interior delight than it did in the beginning before entering the night of sense." Here we experience

God's love and joyfully serve others. The threat in this plateau period is that we may choose to remain there, content with its comforts.

The Father then leads prepared souls into the second dark night—the dark night of the spirit—which uncovers false images of God, false beliefs, and fixation on religious feelings and experiences. Gerald May observes that "we easily become so attached to feelings *of* and *about* God that we equate them *with* God," adding that "this is perhaps the most common idolatry of the spiritual life." In the night of the spirit God causes spiritual comforts to dry up so that the soul feels painfully abandoned. This second dark night—which can continue for months or years—constitutes an invitation to live by radical trust in the absence of spiritual comforts.

In the *active* night of the spirit we clear our minds and spirits of false ideas and limited means of knowing God. John of the Cross insisted that the intellect must be purged of its tendency to fixate on facts about God rather than to know God himself intimately. Furthermore, during this time God breaks the stubborn self-will that blocks the flow of the Spirit. "We would have achieved nothing by purging the intellect and memory in order to ground them in the virtues of faith and hope had we neglected the purification of the will through charity." In the active night of the spirit we purify our spirits by practicing

Divine abandonment "is like the love between a husband and a wife that always remains, even though the husband sometimes has to leave his wife for a time. As a result, the two all the more intensely feel their love for one another. So it is with Christ, who . . . withdraws from the church for a short time. Yet his love continues to burn with love for her."

JOHANNES HOORNBEECK

moral virtues and supplementing verbal prayer with contemplative prayer.

The *passive* night of the spirit represents the most severe yet
significant phase of the soul's purification. Like the sun being ob-
scured by a dark cloud, so the light of God is extinguished in this
phase. The perceived absence of God leaves saints feeling woefully
abandoned. "What the sorrowing soul feels most is the conviction
that God has rejected it, and with abhorrence cast it into darkness.
The thought that God has abandoned it is a piteous and heavy affliction for the soul." During the passive night of the spirit—which
also can last for months or years—we experience difficulty with
prayer and other spiritual exercises. In God's good time our souls
are freed from the dark night to experience the grace of spiritual
marriage and a new level of intimacy with God.

If properly exercised by the dark night, we will emerge more
thoroughly surrendered, purified and united in love with God.
John noted that although many experience the sensory night, "the
spiritual night is the lot of very few, those who have been tried and
are proficient." Those who fail to advance to the night of the spirit
fail to love God and serve others as they ought.

INTERPRETED BY OTHER CHRISTIAN AUTHORITIES

We can learn much from the wisdom of faithful Christian voices
from the past. Martin Luther struggled throughout his life with
demonic attacks that led to seasons of despair and caused him to
question his standing before God. Luther believed that in the mystery of providence, God sometimes afflicts and deserts his saints.
"What, I beseech you, does our Lord God do with his elect? How
strange his guidance by which the elect children of God are led
and governed! Why does he desert and afflict them in this way?"

Swiss Reformer John Calvin also knew the feeling of abandonment by God but saw God as using it for his purposes. "Our most
merciful Father, although he never either sleeps nor idles, still

very often gives the impression of one sleeping or idling in order that he may train us, otherwise, idle and lazy, to seek, ask, and entreat him to our great good."

Finding many examples of the dark night in Scripture, Puritan pastors and theologians described it as a radical form of spiritual depression and the soul's wintertime. Drawing on insights from John of the Cross, Puritans wrote extensively about the distressed soul and the dark nights. They believed that God uses divine desertion to strip away our self-sufficiency and pride. "Among all the works of God's eternal counsel there is nothing more wonderful than His desertion: which is nothing else but an action of God forsaking His creature—that is, by taking away the grace and operation of His Spirit from His creature."

The Puritans insisted that God deserts only Christians, not unbelievers. The Presbyterian preacher Thomas Manton taught that spiritual desertion happens only to the godly; believers living obedient lives may find themselves temporarily walking in darkness. However, those who have never felt the love of Christ will not experience it. "When a child of God is truly walking in God's ways, and when his witness is wholly pleasing unto God, yet still God may withhold His light from His child: and that, they felt, was a most serious and dreadful thing to experience." In his treatise *A Child of Light Walking in Darkness*, Thomas Goodwin wrote, "One who truly fears God, and is obedient to him, may be in a condition of darkness, and have no light; and he may walk many days and years in that condition."

Pastor and spiritual writer A. W. Tozer described the dark night as an "inward death" and an "experience of self crucifixion." He reasoned, "If we cooperate with God He will take away the natural comforts which have served us as mother and nurse for so long and put us where we can receive no help except from the Comforter Himself." Tozer added, "The value of the stripping experience lies in its power to detach us from life's passing interests and to throw us back upon eternity. It serves to empty our earthly vessels and prepare us for the inpouring of the Holy Spirit."

Other leading Christians who shed light on the dark night include the following:

- William Bridge. The English nonconformist pastor noted that following a period of blessing God often hides his face from the redeemed. Why does God so treat his saints? "Does He not withdraw Himself from them, that He may draw them to Himself? Does He not hide his face for a moment that He may not turn His back upon them forever? Does He not forsake them for a moment, that they may die unto the way of sense, and learn to live by faith, which is the proper work of this life?"

- John Bunyan. *The Pilgrim's Progress* portrays Christian's experience in the Valley of the Shadow of Death as "a dark and dismal state." Bunyan added, "Over the Valley hang the discouraging clouds of confusion. . . . In a word, it is dreadful in every way, being utterly without order." Bunyan judged that passage through the Valley of darkness is an inevitable part of the pilgrim's journey to the Celestial City.

- *Westminster Confession of Faith* (1646). Chapter eighteen of this influential Reformed document acknowledges the reality of the soul's dark night as a result of God's deliberate distancing of himself. It reads: "The assurance true believers have of their salvation may be shaken, lessened, or interrupted for various reasons: from committing a particular sin; or *from God's withdrawing the sense of His presence and allowing them to walk in darkness*" (italics added).

- François Fénelon. As for why God absents himself in the dark night, the French spiritual authority wrote, "We suffer from an excessive attachment to the world—above all to self. God orders a series of events which detach us gradually from the world first, and finally from the self also. . . . If the flesh were sound, the surgeon would not need to probe it. He uses the knife only in proportion to the depth of the wound and the extent of proud flesh."

- Pietists. Leaders of the nineteenth-century German Awakening (precursors of the modern evangelical movement) acknowledged the reality of the dark night. In his sermon "The Blessing of Dark Hours in the Christian Life," Friedrich Tholuck described the dark night as that season in which God hides his face and Satan reveals his. This Pietist found a leading example of the dark night in Peter's cowardly denial of Christ. He wrote, "O, you saints and beloved of God . . . see what blessing your dark hours can also achieve for the Savior."

Summing up, the late Christian psychiatrist Gerald May helpfully defined the dark night as follows. "The dark night . . . is an ongoing spiritual process in which we are liberated from spiritual attachments and compulsions and empowered to live and love more freely." He added, "The dark night of the soul is a totally loving, healing, and liberating process. Whether it *feels* that way is another question entirely."

AN EVANGELICAL ASSESSMENT OF THE DARK NIGHT

John, a fortysomething doctoral student of mine, pastored a church on the West Coast. Sensing the complacency of his church body, John prayerfully proposed a plan for spiritual renewal. Committed to the status quo, elders dug in their heels. "Toe the line or you're toast like the three previous pastors," the head elder replied. Several months later the church fired John, who remained unemployed for more than two years. During this painful season God appeared distant, and heaven shut. Having given his best to shepherd the flock, John became bitter toward the church and angry with God. This difficult time, however, prompted John to intensify his pursuit of God. Eventually the Spirit brought John to a place of brokenness, and in the months to follow John experienced spiritual and emotional healing.

For many Christians in our consumer-driven culture the dark night of the soul is unfamiliar territory. When we experience a dark night we're at a loss to explain it. How could a good God withdraw from his children the sense of his presence and blessing? Why should we play by his rules when God appears to desert us? Many are reluctant to admit experiencing dryness and darkness of soul for fear that others will judge us as disobedient or unfaithful.

On my faith journey, as indicated earlier, I have experienced seasons of distress and disorientation, and an occasional dark night of the soul as classically understood. In the following I want to summarize the nature of the dark night as outlined in Scripture and Christian tradition. The dark night of the soul is a painful trial in which we no longer experience spiritual comforts but rather the painful sense of God's absence. Some Christian authorities speak of divine desertion, describing the dark night as an experience where "God has moved away and left no forwarding address." I prefer to describe it as our *perception* of God's absence rather than his actual desertion, because God is always present with his people, even if we do not always feel his comforting presence.

The dark night can be an experience of crisis in a believer's faith. It involves a season of emptiness, disorientation and longing in which God performs spiritual surgery on the soul, shattering the old self and reforming the new. The child of God in the dark night may experience an inability to pray, difficulty hearing the Word of God and a loss of spiritual comforts. Spiritual practices that once brought us near to God no longer seem to work. We may even question the reality of our faith and God's care for us.

Often significant spiritual growth occurs during dark nights as the old self dies away to make room for the new. Developmental psychologist Daniel J. Levinson observed, "Both generativity and its opposite pole, stagnation, are vital to a man's development. To become generative, a man must know how it feels to stagnate—to have the sense of not growing, of being static, stuck, drying up, bogged down in a life full of obligation and devoid of self-fulfillment. He must know the experience of dying, of living in the shadow of death."

Through the dark night, then, God changes the habits of our lives, lovingly weaning us from attachment to inordinate pleasures, possessions and puffed-up egos. He cuts away at our spiritual greed in which we seek pleasurable comforts more than God himself. When our hearts are devoted to anything other than the true God, we worship false gods. Through the distress of the dark night God detaches soul and spirit from these lesser loyalties and nudges us toward maturity in Christ.

Our Lord taught as much in John 15:1-8, where the gardener prunes fruit-bearing branches back to the stem so they might produce quality fruit of lasting value. Kathleen Norris points out, "The point of our crises and calamities is not to frighten us or beat us into submission but to encourage us to change, to allow us to heal and grow." Just like in a marriage, hard times in life highlight our need to mature. Challenging seasons prompt the exchange of romantic love rooted in pleasurable feelings for *agapē* love rooted in truth, commitment and service to the other.

The dark night of the soul is a fitting instance of what the Princeton pastoral theologian James Loder calls a "transforming moment." We see an example of this moment of awakening and empowerment in Christ when Saul encounters the Savior on the road to Damascus or when Cleopas and the other disciples engage the risen Lord at their table. The transforming moment leads to *convictional knowing*, to engaging the truth about God and ourselves in the deepest part of our souls. Convictional knowing (knowing *who*) does not contradict analytical knowing (knowing *about*), but it proves far richer. In this life-changing moment, God

leads us to repentance, and we experience a deeper level of healing and transformation. We also have a better understanding of
ourselves (even though it remains incomplete in this life). According to Daniel Levinson, distressing life occurrences that produce
constructive change are "crucial
marker events" in our lives.

> "Anyone who talks about
> spiritual things without any
> experience in them is like a
> person who is lost in the desert,
> dying with thirst. . . .
> If you try to tell me about the
> Christian life without any
> personal involvement in it,
> you will mislead me.
> You will tell me fictional
> things, mistaken things."
>
> PSEUDO-MACARIUS

The dark night of the soul may be
brought on by an external event such
as loss of a job, failure of a career,
breakup of a marriage or religious
persecution. Internal factors such as
debilitating disease, emotional breakdown or a painful midlife transition
can cause it. The dark night could
also accompany movement across a
major boundary of the spiritual journey. Ultimately, however, the dark
night results from God's intentional
action whereby he purifies our
fleshly natures. The ambiguity and
distress we experience highlight our
sinful passions, lack of spiritual pursuit and desperate need for God.

Through the dark night God can
do his greatest work in us. The com-
passionate God leads us through desert places in order to refresh
us with the water of life and feed us with the bread of life. As Moses said to the Israelites in the wilderness, "The LORD your God . . .
humbled you, causing you to hunger and then feeding you with
manna, which neither you nor your ancestors had known, to teach
you that people do not live on bread alone but on every word that
comes from the mouth of the LORD" (Deut 8:2-3). Gerald May comments regarding the dark night, "Maybe, sometimes, in the midst

of things going terribly wrong, something is going just right."

By analogy, some plants grow only in the shade, not in full sunlight. Some vegetation flourishes in the bottom of the ocean in virtual darkness. Moreover, we revel at the stars in the heavens not in the light of the day but during the dark of night. Indeed, the darker the night, the more brilliantly the stars shine. Similarly, the darkest moments of our soul provide the greatest potential for transformation. Saints who sink to the depths are empowered to rise to the heights.

The turmoil of the dark night, however, can pose a threat if we fail to respond properly. Overcome with confusion, we might conclude that God is not there for us—that God has not come to our aid in a time of dire need. We may be tempted to flee the darkness, rail at God, drop out of the church or seek worldly pleasures to fill our emptiness.

A church, parachurch or other organization may experience what might be called a corporate dark night. A Christian community may suffer the same spirit of confusion and dryness as an individaul experiencing his or her dark night. The Spiritual Formation Forum recently highlighted churches in Minnesota and California that went into a spiritual funk and lost membership before recapturing their zeal for God through renewing disciplines of spiritual formation.

As twenty-first-century Christians, we must properly apply John of the Cross's portrayal of the dark night of the soul to our times so that we can learn the most from the experience. Henri

> *"Deliverance can come to us only by the defeat of our old life. . . .*
>
> *God rescues us by breaking us, by shattering our strength and wiping out our resistance.*
>
> *Then He invades our natures with that ancient and eternal life which is from the beginning."*
>
> A. W. TOZER

Nouwen cautions that in the process of dying to old attachments we may "end up with too many noes" that frustrate soul and spirit. These include "no to your former way of thinking and feeling, no to things you did in the past, and most of all, no to human relationships that were once precious and life-giving." As we seek a balanced posture between strictness and joy, and between negation and the celebration of life as God's good gift, we believers today can still enjoy loyal friends, tasty food, inspiring music and the beauty of God's creation. But we can also learn a great deal from the main features of the dark night as identified by John of the Cross, most importantly that we must not love anything, however good and beautiful, that keeps us from loving Jesus "more than these" (Jn 21:15).

THE DARK NIGHT AND CLINICAL DEPRESSION

Because believers sometimes experience a dark night and a depressive episode simultaneously, Scripture and Christian history suggest a relationship between the dark night of the soul and clinical depression. The sense of God's absence from our lives, for example, can afflict the soul with despondency and depression. Conversely, depressed hearts darken the bright light of God's presence. However, the dark night and depression may be distinguished. As put by Thomas Moore, "depression is a psychological sickness, a dark night is a spiritual trial."

The dark night of the soul differs from clinical depression in several respects. Depression is often characterized by diminished effectiveness in work, a high degree of self-absorption and withdrawal, and may be eased by leisure activities and medical intervention. A depressed person, moreover, typically pleads for help. The dark night of the soul, on the other hand, involves little loss of efficiency in work and is not substantially eased by recreational diversions and medical treatment. People in a dark night usually do not withdraw from life, and they often exude compassion for others. Unlike depression, the dark night is a holy-ground experience resulting in spiritual transformation. We often sense the reality of God's wisdom and goodness in the company of a person experiencing a dark night. "In spite of everything, there is an underlying sense of rightness in the Dark Night."

John of the Cross proposed at least three signs that differentiate a dark night of the soul from other potential causes of darkness in our lives, such as living in sin, melancholia or a physical illness. The first sign of the dark night: a person undergoing a dark night finds minimal consolation in God. Next, even though the soul may be cast down, a dark night sufferer intensely desires to reconnect with God. Finally, the person in a dark night cannot meditate on the things of God like he or she used to. Through the painful dark night, John insisted, God is preparing the soul for deeper prayer of contemplation.

TRANSFORMATIONAL OUTCOMES OF THE DARK NIGHT

Let's review what we have learned so far. The dark night, first of all, creates a sensory and spiritual vacuum that highlights our inherent sinfulness. In the state of spiritual darkness we see with greater clarity our true selves, our deepest needs and our hidden sins.

> *"The first and chief benefit that this dry and dark night of contemplation causes is the knowledge of self and of one's own misery."*
>
> JOHN OF THE CROSS

The opaqueness of the night brings into clearer focus the soul's poverty, in the form of self-seeking, self-love and self-sufficiency. As Thomas Moore put it, "A dark night of the soul takes you to Hell, where you not only feel withdrawn from life, you also discover your own perversity and dark inclinations."

The dark night impels an intentional quest for God. The psalmist mused, "When I was in distress, I sought the Lord" (Ps 77:2). Dutiful prayers of an earlier period give way to prayers of urgency, if not

> "When God's countenance is hid, the fountain of life is darkened, and so a general darkness befalls them. Then the heart is driven to God and God delights to restore and comfort a man again."
>
> THOMAS GOODWIN

desperation. The distressing dark night leads us to surrender our lives unconditionally to God. We thus come to know God in a new way, moving from knowing *about* God at an intellectual level to knowing God relationally from the heart. With regard to Bernard of Clairvaux's journey model (see appendix), the darkness redirects believers from the second stage, "love of God for self," to the third stage, "love of God for God."

Through the ambiguity of the dark night God purifies and transforms our old, fleshly nature. John of the Cross likened God's love to a fire that dries out a log, sets it aflame and transforms it. In *The Living Flame of Love* he wrote, "The dark fire of God is His remedy and medicine, which He gives to the soul to treat its many diseases. He does so, only to bring the soul back to health . . . to drive from it every kind if spiritual evil." The fire of the night reforms our hearts with humility and purity to make us more like Christ. "In the dark night something of your make-up comes to an end—your ego, your self, your creativeness, your meaning. You may find in that darkness a key to your source, the larger soul that makes you who you are."

The trial of the dark night loosens our habit of clinging to religious feelings and ecstatic experiences. Transformation comes from God directly speaking, not from emotional highs. As John of the Cross insightfully observed, "Delightful feelings do not of themselves lead the soul to God, but rather cause it to become attached to delightful feelings." The dark night strips whatever objects or thrills supplant God in our lives and frees us from inferior loyalties in order to deepen love and heighten joy. The prophet Isaiah stated that God gave Israel "the bread of adversity and the water of affliction" as means of turning wayward hearts to himself (Is 30:20).

Seasons of God's hiddenness call saints to follow Jesus at all costs regardless of the blessings we do or do not experience. When things are going smoothly, we take charge of our life, but when our path is shrouded in darkness we have no alternative but to trust God unconditionally. This makes good sense, for what is visible requires little need for faith. The times of darkness invite us to trust in God under all circumstances.

> *"God who is everywhere never leaves us. . . . Yet he may be more present to us when he is absent than when he is present."*
>
> THOMAS MERTON

The dark night gives us the chance to take up Christ's cross and share in his sufferings. It enables us to participate in Christ's betrayal and pain. Apostle Paul had this end in mind when he contemplated believers filling up the sufferings of Christ (Col 1:24). Peter added, "Rejoice inasmuch as you participate in the sufferings of Christ" (1 Pet 4:13). Jesus drank the cup of desolation when forsaken on the cross, "and that cup hath gone around among God's people every since." The late Pope John Paul II encouraged those distressed by serious afflictions to "join their suffering to Christ's."

The dark night does not alter our past history, our personality structure or our DNA. But it does radically strip away the old self and its passions, reconfiguring the new self in Christ. As we cooperate with God's mysterious work, the darkness of the night can become a definitive formational experience on our faith journeys.

FOR INDIVIDUAL OR GROUP REFLECTION AND DISCUSSION

1. After reading this chapter, in what ways has your understanding

of the dark night of the soul and its spiritually renewing outcomes been clarified or enlarged?

2. What idol have you been holding on to that prevents you from yielding your life completely to God? What role is this attachment filling in your life that God should be filling?

3. Is Jesus truly sufficient for all your needs? Can you let go of your inferior, restricting attachments and confess that Jesus alone is enough?

5 *Painful Disorientation*

Redemptive Responses

"Therefore, my dear friends . . .
continue to work out your salvation
with fear and trembling, for it is God
who works in you to will and to act
in order to fulfill his good purpose."

PHILIPPIANS 2:12-13

Wⁿᵉⁿ **W**hile ministering in a retreat setting, I met Beth, a thirty-something, musically gifted graduate of a prestigious university. After initial enthusiasm as a Christian, Beth entered a season of spiritual dryness and confusion. Friends responded by saying, "You're not reading the Bible consistently" and "You're not spending sufficient time in prayer." Beth consulted a spiritual mentor who encouraged her to spend time in a renewal community known for its formational ministry. Beth took a six-month leave of absence from her job and joined the community as a volunteer. Her spiritual director encouraged Beth to keep her daily appointments with God regardless of her feelings. She also guided her in the practice of spiritual disciplines such as *lectio divina*, listening to God and keeping a spiritual journal. Beth also participated in a spiritual formation group where members processed their spiritual journeys and supported one another with encouragement and prayer. Within a few months Beth's relationship with God was renewed and her life revitalized.

In this chapter we consider how we can constructively respond to painful seasons of darkness and disorientation. What can we do—what ought we do—when we find ourselves spiritually distressed or perhaps encased in a dark night? For starters, there is no magic formula or prescribed number of steps that with certainty will ease our distresses. We must, however, be proactive and take appropriate action. We can err in several ways: by becoming passive and assuming that God will work things out apart from our participation, by taking matters into our own hands and leaving God out of the equation, or by abandoning hope and sliding into a spiral of despair.

GOD AND DISCIPLES: EACH DOING OUR PART
God works in every circumstance of life—pleasant and painful—to transform his people and advance his kingdom. As Jesus said to Jewish leaders, "My Father is always at his work to this very day, and I too am working" (Jn 5:17). The loving Father wills that we join with him to bring to fruition his redemptive purposes. Paul stressed that while God works for our salvation, we also have to do our part. Peter also showed that we each play a part, citing both God's provisions sufficient for a godly life (2 Pet 1:3) and our necessary responses (2 Pet 1:5-8). Augustine acknowledged this divine-human synergy by suggesting that without God we can accomplish

nothing, but without us neither will God work in our lives.

Jean Pierre de Caussade (1675-1751) coined the phrase "sacrament of the present moment," meaning that Christ works his purposes through our decisions and actions in the nitty-gritty of everyday life. Caussade believed that the trials we endure conceal God's active work in the give-and-take of life. Notwithstanding our hardships and struggles, we can be comforted by the fact that "what he ordains for us each moment is what is most holy, best and most divine for us." In seasons of distress and darkness, if we want to triumph amidst trials, we must faithfully do our part and then leave the outcome to God.

> *"Grace is opposed to earning, not to effort. And it is well-directed, decisive and sustained effort that is the key to the Kingdom and to the life of restful power in ministry and life."*
>
> DALLAS WILLARD

Doing our part means that we will attend to our physical, emotional and spiritual worlds. In *The House of the Soul* Evelyn Underhill likened the Christian life to a two-story house. The lower floor represents a well-ordered natural life of moderation and endurance. The upper floor represents a prayerfully nurtured spiritual life. On our journeys, she insisted, we must cultivate both our physical and emotional worlds, and our spiritual world. With this in mind, how might we cooperate with God's providential purposes for our lives? What pieces of spiritual armor must we put on to prosper on our spiritual journeys? Scripture and spiritual authorities offer guidance as to how we can respond to manage our trials, grow and bear much fruit. To these we now turn.

TURN FROM ALL KNOWN SIN

We must first examine the condition of our hearts. Sin is a root cause (not the only one) of anguish and pain. Sins invite subjective guilt that casts a cloud over our hearts. Because God, who is radiant light, cannot fellowship with darkness, we must admit our wrongs, repent of them and cast off sin. The psalmist mused:

> Who may ascend the mountain of the LORD?
>> Who may stand in his holy place?
> Those who have clean hands and a pure heart,
>> who do not put their trust in an idol
>> or swear by a false god. (Ps 24:3-4)

In the Sermon on the Mount Jesus taught, "Blessed are the pure in heart, for they will see God" (Mt 5:8; see also Heb 12:14). We are able to "see" the Lord in personal and corporate worship when we have confessed and repented of all known sin.

We must also receive the forgiveness God freely offers. Some saints experience difficulty accepting God's pardon; often we find it easier to forgive others than to forgive ourselves. We trample on God's grace when we refuse to forgive ourselves after he has forgiven us. C. S. Lewis observed that when we fail to forgive ourselves after Christ has forgiven us, we establish ourselves as a higher judge than God himself—which cannot be. According to Thelma Hall, "Our sense of unworthiness is a subtle form of arrogance, whereby we choose not to forgive the one whom God has forgiven." We do well to practice the converse of the Golden Rule: to do unto ourselves as we do to others. In order to embrace God's forgiveness I have found it helpful to receive the assurance of forgiveness from a minister, priest or other person in a position of spiritual authority.

> *"It is highly unfitting that the sanctuary in which he [Christ] dwells should be like a stable crammed with filth."*
>
> JOHN CALVIN

God enjoins those who would walk in his ways to travel the "Highway of Holiness" (Is 35:8 NLT). The New Testament reiterates this moral obligation: "God did not call us to be impure, but to live a holy life" (1 Thess 4:7). Fellowship with Christ requires that we walk circumspectly and uprightly. Barna research reports that only 55 percent of born-again people indicate that they know someone whom they would describe as holy. The Christian community needs to recover a passion for holiness as called for in Holy Scripture.

While a student in seminary I was asked to preach a sermon at a missions conference on discerning God's will for one's life. Being young and inexperienced I asked my preaching professor for a suggested text on which to base my sermon. Without hesitation he recommended 1 Thessalonians 4:3, 7, which reads: "It is God's will that you should be sanctified. . . . For God did not call us to be impure, but to live a holy life." God grants grace to overcome our trials if our hearts are obedient and chaste.

I know a godly psychiatrist who has practiced for decades. When distressed people seek his help, the psychiatrist begins not with insights from Freud or Jung but with the simple question "Is there any unconfessed sin in your life?" He knows that cherished sins block the flow of God's love and conflict the heart with anxiety and remorse.

Often we are our own worst enemies. We must, therefore, bring every sin into the light of God's grace. Pleading Christ's perfect righteousness, we receive the Father's forgiveness. Dis-

> *"The vigor and power of the spiritual life depend upon the mortification of sin."*
>
> JOHN OWEN

tressed souls, of course, need to put their sense of sin in perspective. Excessive sorrow for sin that abandons hope of God's pardon is itself sin. As noted by the Puritan Richard Sibbes, "The soul is cast down too much . . . *when our mourning and sorrow bring us not to God, but drive us from God*. Grief, sorrow and humility are good; but discouragement is evil."

BE ASSURED OF GOD'S LOVINGKINDNESS

Nothing uplifts our hearts more than knowing that we are loved.
The Lord who knows us completely loves us deeply, even in our
confusion and doubt. Through the course of his troublesome journey David reassured himself of God's unfailing love:

> The LORD is compassionate and gracious,
> slow to anger, abounding in love. . . .
> He does not treat us as our sins deserve
> or repay us according to our iniquities.
> For as high as the heavens are above the earth,
> so great is his love for those who fear him. (Ps 103:8, 10-11)

Faith looks beyond the tears and trusts that the loving God
hears our cry, knows our distress and will come to our aid.

When troubled or afflicted, we can be confident that the thorn
represents a circumstance ordained for our ultimate good. Knowing
that God is working in our lives through hardship sustains us in that
distress. The loving Father has not brought us this far on the journey
to abandon us. As we ponder God's lovingkindness, mercy and faithfulness, our hearts are strengthened for the challenges we face.

The loving Father knows our limits and will not permit us to be
afflicted beyond our capacity, however severely we feel we're being
pushed to the wall. Paul reminds us, "God is faithful; he will not
let you be tempted beyond what you can bear. But when you are
tempted, he will also provide a way out so that you can endure it"
(1 Cor 10:13). God may bend the reed in order to strengthen it, but
assuredly he will not break it (Is 42:3). During a difficult stage of
my journey recently, I discovered to my great delight that God
provided exactly the resources I needed at precisely the right time.
Like Israel wandering in the desert, God supplied manna sufficient for the day. Thus when darkness obscures the Father's love
and dims hope, let's make Job's sturdy commitment our own:
"Though he slay me, yet will I hope in him" (Job 13:15).

EXPRESS FEELINGS OF DISTRESS TO GOD

An essential component of healing is to bare our soul by freely sharing with God our deepest longings and hurts. Sin loses its power over us when we're aware of it and acknowledge it before him. God lovingly longs for us to honestly share our deepest concerns with him. Far from displaying an emotionless, grin-and-bear-it attitude, we must bring all our feelings of disappointment and grief to God. As spiritual guide Friedrich von Hügel put it, "Gently turn to Him your love and life, and tell Him gently that you want Him and all of Him: and that you beg for courage." God is not put off by our pleas for assistance. Rather, he enthusiastically welcomes our heartfelt expressions of need.

Psalmists of old cried out to the Lord with earnest entreaties.

> I cry aloud to the LORD;
>   I lift up my voice to the LORD for mercy.
> I pour out before him my complaint;
>   before him I tell my trouble. (Ps 142:1-2)

Suppressing our true feelings deadens our souls and deepens our distress. We draw comfort as we express our heartfelt longings in words of painful disorientation akin to those found in Psalms 69, 77 and 88. After honestly unburdening our hearts, we can relax and allow the compassionate God to accomplish his renewing work.

ABANDON ALL TO GOD

Seek! When we're distressed we often pursue God with sincere, heartfelt longing. "My heart says of you, 'Seek his face!' / Your face, LORD, I will seek" (Ps 27:8). When we're honest before God about our struggles and uncertainties, he honors our sincere questioning. David often sought the Lord when he was weary and troubled.

> From the ends of the earth I call to you,
>   I call as my heart grows faint;
>   lead me to the rock that is higher than I. (Ps 61:2)

As we seek after God we can be assured that all the while he has been seeking after us. If we seek him persistently with pure intention, we surely will find him.

Surrender! Through disorienting seasons of our lives God invites us not to self-loathing but to submission. When life caves in we commit ourselves completely to the One to whom we rightly belong. C. S. Lewis pointed out the danger of failing to surrender: "God cannot bless us unless He has us. When we try to keep within us an area that is our own, we try to keep an area of death." The peace Jesus gave to us, his apprentices, requires that we fall into the arms of the Savior with complete abandonment. As we submit to God fully he blesses us with his calming presence.

> *"It takes me a long time to realize that God has no respect for anything I bring Him. All He wants from me is unconditional surrender."*
>
> OSWALD CHAMBERS

Surrender simply means that we release all our weight into the Father's loving arms, much as a baby rests contentedly in its mother's arms. Securely held in his loving embrace, we permit the master Potter to have his way with us, the clay. Catherine of Genoa (1447-1510) thought that she had to give God the "keys to my house" so that Christ's transforming work would become fully present. With each act of surrender another layer of the distrust peels away. Admittedly, surrender to God is threatening because it involves forfeiting control of our lives. It feels like jumping off a cliff without a safety tether. But only by surrendering unreservedly to God do we become the whole and fruitful people he wants us to be.

C. S. Lewis made this point well: "Christ says, 'Give me All. I don't want so much of your time and so much of your money and so much of your work: I want you. I have not come to torment your natural self, but to kill it. . . . I will give you a new self instead. In fact, I will give you Myself: my own will shall become yours.'" Faith grasps the paradox that the more we surrender to Christ the more of him we gain in return.

Trust! Heartbreaking circumstances represent graced opportunities to trust. When we cannot manage life's trials on our own, we turn to the One we know is our only source of help. God is pleased when we trust him in all the seasons of our lives— peaceful and turbulent. As God said to Israel of old,

"Abandonment is practiced by continually losing your own will in the will of God; by plunging your will into the depths of His will, there to be lost forever!"

JEANNE GUYON

> Let those who walk in the dark,
>   who have no light,
> trust in the name of the LORD
>   and rely on their God. (Is 50:10)

As we received the gift of eternal life by faith, the same faith will see us through our challenging life journeys here below (see Col 2:6).

We trust in God's unshakable Word rather than our fickle feelings, which ebb and flow like the tides of the sea. Even in the darkness, we obey God in every area of our lives by seeking to follow the directives in his Word and the leading of his Spirit. As the psalmist testified, "These words hold me up in bad times; / yes, your promises rejuvenate me" (Ps 119:50 *The Message*).

Some years ago a young friend of mine in Christian service was diagnosed with a life-threatening brain tumor. As we brought meals to Dan and his wife, my friend was visibly distraught. I quietly prayed that the Spirit would give me a word of encouragement to share with him. The Lord prompted me to embrace my friend and say, "Dan, I believe God invites you to surrender yourself completely and unreservedly to our loving Lord and his purpose for your life. He is utterly faithful and will grant you his very best." After brain surgery Dan confounded the doctors by his recovery from the cancer, and he is clear of the disease to this day.

Wait! When we're perplexed or distressed we have to wait on God, never doubting that he is working out his will. As a young Christian I recall being confused about what waiting on the Lord meant, and I still sometimes struggle with the need to patiently wait for his perfect timing. But I now understand that waiting on the Lord is about faith being extended as long as is required to ensure the unfolding of God's will. Exercised by his personal dark night, Martin Marty spoke of waiting as "the key element in a wintry sort of spirituality." As the anxious psalmist put it:

> I wait for the LORD, my whole being waits,
>   and in his word I put my hope.
> I wait for the LORD
>   more than watchmen wait for the morning,
>   more than watchmen wait for the morning. (Ps 130:5-6)

Waiting reminds us that we cannot force God's hand; we can only tarry with hearts at rest, trusting his timely response. We wait on the Lord with patience because God is not driven by haste to accomplish his purposes. Restoration of body and soul typically occurs not overnight but over time. But as we wait, we take refuge in God, who is our safe haven.

"My spirit has become dry because it forgets to feed on You."

JOHN OF THE CROSS

Listen! Listening attentively to God is a neglected spiritual practice in our hectic, multitasking culture. The Lord is ever present to his people, but our lives are so cluttered with busyness and noise that we often fail to hear his voice. From personal experience I have discovered that God rarely communicates by a bolt of lightening or a clap of thunder. Typically he communicates through gentle nudging of the Spirit. When Elijah fled into the desert following his dramatic victory over 850 false prophets on Mount Carmel, God came to the distraught prophet not through powerful wind, earthquake or fire, but in a "a gentle and quiet whisper" (1 Kings 19:12 *The Message*).

> *"Every time you listen to the voice [of God] that calls you the Beloved, you will discover within yourself a desire to hear that voice longer and more deeply. It is like discovering a well in the desert."*
>
> HENRI NOUWEN

To hear God's voice rather than our own confused inner voices, we have to find quiet spaces where we can simply be present and listen. We can be confident that it is Jesus who speaks to us, for his sheep instinctively know the Shepherd's voice. With hearts so attuned we can discern his encouragement and direction for our lives. Mother Teresa put it well: God "cannot be found in noise and restlessness. God is the friend of silence. See how nature—trees, flowers, grass—grow in silence. See the stars, the moon and sun, how they move in silence. . . . The more we [hear and] receive in silent prayer, the more we can give in our active life."

RECOGNIZE THE VALUE OF SUFFERING IN THE DIVINE ECONOMY

A fundamental truth of the spiritual life is that to become like Jesus we must be formed by testing and trials. The path to maturity in Christ passes more through thickets of thorns than through beds of roses. As much as we dislike and resist it, suffering is one of the primary means God employs to nurture us in godliness. The hard truth, as François Fénelon put it, is that God "has had to bring us low through trials; he has had to crush our pride; he has

"Afflictions and the

cauterizations of the flesh burn

away the rust of sin and perfect

the life of the just."

ANSELM OF CANTERBURY

had to baffle our fleshly wisdom; he has had to dismay our vaunted self-worth." As we submit to God in our trials, he turns our anguish into eternal good.

From his many years of physical suffering Friedrich von Hügel concluded, "Remember, no joy without suffering—no patience without trial—no humility without humiliation—no life without death." Remember that Jesus' disciples followed the *crucified* Lord, and so do we. Our pain and suffering are essential to our identification with Jesus, who himself "learned obedience from what he suffered" (Heb 5:8). If during his earthly life the Son of God needed to grow in obedience through trials, how much more do we? To become like Jesus we must join our suffering to his. Our task, however, is not merely to endure suffering, but to embrace it, find God in it and draw closer to him through it. Simply put, "There is no remedy for this darkness but to sink into it."

JOURNEY TO ONE'S "INNER SINAI"

Before launching into uncharted territory we must first seek to understand our inner self. Under the pressure of multiple obligations we tend to live on life's outer boundary, occupied with visible and tangible concerns. Life's stressors often tear us away from our spiritual home, but for transformation to occur we must launch an intentional journey inward to our deepest center, or "interior Sinai," as Augustine put it. Christendom's leading theologian urged, "Do not go abroad. Return within yourself. In the inward man swells truth." We tend to resist a serious journey inward because it can be emotionally and spiritually unsettling as we engage unhealed areas of the soul. To our detriment, Protestants tend to overlook the necessity of an intentional and disciplined journey to our interior world.

Journeying inward will require slowing our lives down. I've already quoted this but it's worth hearing again: "A certain slowing down and spacing out of our ceaseless activities is a necessary condition of the deepening and enrichment of life. The spirit of Joy and the spirit of Hurry cannot live in the same house." I have discovered that when I travel inward (without, of course, becoming self-absorbed) I experience a double blessing. First, I acquire self-knowledge (the truth about myself) and self-understanding (awareness of my credits and deficits); I discover

"Blessed is the man who knows his own weakness, because this knowledge becomes for him the foundation, the root, and the beginning of all goodness."

ISAAC THE SYRIAN

more of who I really am and ultimately find my true identity in Jesus Christ. Second, I connect with Christ, who dwells at the center of my being. Jesus lives in us and patiently waits for our hearts to cling to his.

On the journey inward we might find areas of unforgiveness, woundedness and guilt. But with grace, God peels off the layers of our old self, making us more whole. In this process, it also helps to pay careful attention to dreams that reveal crucial aspects of the self buried in our unconscious. We might even seek the counsel of a godly friend to help discern the meaning of our dreams.

Talk-show host and author Dennis Prager wisely asked, "Who is likely to be psychologically deeper—the person who devotes time and effort to learning about herself/himself or the one who rarely looks within?" He added, "Pursuing depth is one of the distinguishing characteristics of the human being; it is one of the noblest goals of a human life; and it brings ongoing happiness."

We journey to our inner Sinai to know God more intimately by practicing healthy spiritual habits. Spiritual disciplines are prac-

"Possibly our society will be wrecked because it is completely taken up with externals and has no grasp on this inner dimension of life."

THOMAS MERTON

tices that form us spiritually and foster fellowship with God. Henri Nouwen insightfully observed that "we cannot organize or manipulate God. But without careful discipline we cannot receive Him either."

For Protestants who stress God's free grace (apart from human effort), practicing spiritual disciplines may require a paradigm shift. The benefits of edifying spiritual disciplines far exceed the effort invested. Consider the spiritual athleticism of godly souls such as John the Baptist in the wilderness, Jesus fasting for forty days in the desert and Paul disciplining his body into submission. To transform us into Christlikeness the Spirit uses disciplines such as formative reading of the Scriptures *(lectio divina),* corporate worship, solitude, prayer, fasting, taking retreats and keeping a spiritual journal. The discipline of daily meeting with God is crucial to navigating through a dark night of the soul.

Prayer lies at the heart of the journey to our inner Sinai. In difficult times we may feel resistant toward praying, but we must direct our wills to pray as much as we can, with God's help. As we lift our hearts to God in prayer, we know that he hears us (1 Jn 5:14), even though he might not answer immediately or as we wish. Should God not answer when or how we'd like him to, it's because his perfect wisdom has something better in mind for us. Be assured that he loves us and is committed to care for us.

To foster spiritual growth we do well to practice a variety of prayer forms. These might include the prayer of examen, where we review our day to understand how we have pleased or displeased God. Or contemplative prayer, where we lovingly focus on God himself by meditating on his attributes. Or healing prayer, where with the help of others we invite God to bring his healing power to bear on our physical, emotional or spiritual troubles. Since God knows our needs, we do well to supplement the familiar prayer of the lips (petition, intercession) with the prayer of the heart (listening, practicing the Presence). Prayer keeps us connected to the heart of God. The Norwegian spiritual writer Ole Hallesby stated that "prayer is really an attitude of our hearts to God. As such it finds expression, at times in words and at times without words, precisely as when two people love each other." When Paul commanded believers to "pray continually" or "pray all the time" (1 Thess 5:17 *The Message*) he meant for us to continually abide in, love and talk with the lover of our souls.

> *"Prayer means launching out of the heart toward God; a cry of grateful love from the crest of joy or the trough of despair:*
>
> *it is a vast, supernatural force that opens out my heart and binds me close to Jesus."*
>
> THÉRÈSE OF LISIEUX

We can find help for our journey to our inner Sinai by using a rule of life, classically known as an *askesis* (from a Greek word meaning to train or discipline). A rule of life might include practicing two or three short times of prayer daily, writing in a journal several times a week or taking a monthly retreat. Spiritual formation requires spiritual training just as an athlete requires disciplined physical conditioning. Paul wrote, "Do you not know that in a race all the runners run, but only one gets the prize? Everyone who competes in the games goes into strict training. They do it to get a crown that will not last; but we do it to get a crown that will last forever" (1 Cor 9:24-25; see also 2 Tim 2:3-6).

A spiritual rule *(regula)* fosters a lifestyle of discipline that deepens our intimacy with Jesus and transforms our lives. An *askesis* preserves us from spiritual lethargy and the chronic busyness that crowds God out of our worlds. Eugene Peterson helpfully observes that an intentional *askesis* guards against an "involuntary askesis," made necessary, for example, by a serious physical illness, emotional breakdown or relational failure.

> *"The repetition of many particular acts of this loving knowledge becomes so continuous that a habit is formed in the soul."*
>
> JOHN OF THE CROSS

PRAISE GOD FOR PAST MERCIES

God loves a sincerely grateful heart! In the best of times as well as the worst of times we do well to praise the Lord, the Giver and Sustainer of life. A distressed psalmist lamented the apparent absence of God's presence and comforts, but then recalled God's former mercies that brought deliverance: "I will remember the deeds of the LORD; / yes, I will remember your miracles of long ago" (Ps 77:11). When we're downcast we should recall and praise God for his past blessings and favors. God's people of old praised him for rescue from foes, for healing from the ravages of disease and for redemption from the plague of sin.

When I'm facing trying times I find great encouragement from saints of old who praised God in the midst of their challenges. Recalling God's deliverance from past distresses lifts our spirits and strengthens our hearts to overcome present trials. The act of praising God in our sorrow represents the first step toward deliverance. Thus the psalmist mused:

> Why, my soul, are you downcast?
>   Why so disturbed within me?
> Put your hope in God,
>   for I will yet praise him,
>   my Savior and my God. (Ps 42:11)

While we praise God for his rich bounty, we also acknowledge that his ways are beyond our finite comprehension. In the Christian journey we learn to trust God implicitly even though his purposes may at times be clouded in darkness.

Praising God in the midst of our trials also includes clinging to precious promises from the Scriptures. Imitate Job, who amidst overwhelming calamities grasped the promise of a coming Redeemer who would reclaim his life and empower him to see God (Job 19:25-27). Embrace the hope of our spiritual father, Abraham, of whom it is written: "He did not waver through unbelief regarding the promise of God, but was strengthened in his faith and gave glory to God" (Rom 4:20). Meditate on and commit to memory other biblical affirmations of confidence and comfort, such as the following:

> *"It is incredible how efficacious a remedy the praise of God is in times of danger; for as soon as you begin to praise God, the evil lessens, confidence grows, and calling upon God in faith follows."*
>
> MARTIN LUTHER

- "The LORD is good to those whose hope is in him, / to the one who seeks him; / it is good to wait quietly / for the salvation of the LORD" (Lam 3:25-26).

- "For a brief moment I abandoned you, / but with deep compassion I will bring you back" (Is 54:7).

- "'I know the plans I have for you,' declares the LORD, 'plans to prosper you and not to harm you, plans to give you a hope and a future'" (Jer 29:11).

Trusting God's Spirit-inspired promises in Scripture brings hope to our troubled souls. God's pledges are like fresh breezes that disperse the dark clouds of discouragement, pure water that refreshes parched and weary souls, or fine bread that nourishes famished frames. As we trust God's promises, our merciful heavenly friend helps our weary souls, enabling us to bear, indeed even triumph, amidst trials. The greater the discomforts that trouble us, the greater the comforts God dispenses as we wholeheartedly trust him.

"The sacred promises . . . are of no avail for the comfort and sustenance of the soul unless you grasp them by faith, plead them in prayer, expect them by hope, and receive them with gratitude."

CHARLES H. SPURGEON

WALK WITH A SPIRITUAL COMPANION

Western cultures are dominated by individualism and self-reliance. A recent study by the National Opinion Research Center in Chicago states that Americans are "living lonelier, more isolated lives than in the past." The research confirms a shrinking social network in which nearly a quarter of Americans have no close friends. To journey successfully through life's ups and downs, however, we need to partner with a discerning spiritual friend. Through the grace of spiritual companionship we receive a double blessing: the spiritual friend supports us in our struggles, and he or she helps us grow in our relationship with Christ.

The fact that we believers have direct access to Jesus, our great high priest, does not preclude seeking out a human friend to walk with us on our journeys. God designed the church to be a community of supportive brothers and sisters who open their hearts to one another to be formed together in Christ. As we come to intimately know others in the body of the church, we grow in our knowledge of God and his ways. God uses the caring ministry of a spiritual companion to help us confront our demons, heal and grow. Joyfully, I have discovered that I have grown most when walking with a godly spiritual companion or mentor.

Spiritual companionship, or spiritual direction, has a long and fruitful history. Moses, Naomi, Samuel and Paul fruitfully exercised this supportive ministry. The apostle Paul reminded the Corinthian church that "in Christ Jesus I became your father through the gospel" (1 Cor 4:15). Desert fathers and mothers, Gregory the Great, Bernard of Clairvaux, Thomas à Kempis, Martin Luther, Teresa of Ávila, John of the Cross, the Puritan divines and Thomas Merton, to name a few, all provided this caring ministry. Protestant Christians are now rediscovering the life-giving ministry of soul care in our time.

I have found the godly soul friend to be an empathic listener, codiscerner and prayer partner who helps me to respond more authentically to the Spirit's leading. The spiritual companion facilitates deepening relationship with Christ and encourages kingdom living. Many Christian spiritual authorities testified to the dangers of traversing life's pathway without a godly spiritual guide. Bernard of Clairvaux commented, "He who sets himself up as his own teacher becomes the pupil of a fool."

"I am fully persuaded that if you always had one or two faithful friends near you who speak the very truth from their heart and watch over you in love, you would swiftly advance."

JOHN WESLEY

Other spiritual mentors insisted that the gospel life with its twists and turns is too much for us to handle on our own. We need the counsel, guidance and support of others who will walk the path with us. In both good and bad times we do well to abandon our supposed self-sufficiency and walk with a godly spiritual mentor.

Spiritual direction involves the Christian pilgrim disclosing the working of his or her soul to a spiritual friend or mentor. By being honest with our spiritual friend we invite accountability, support and encouragement. Walking with a prayerful spiritual companion helps us pay attention to spiritual impulses at work in our lives whether from God, the sinful flesh or the evil one. The spiritual companion facilitates listening to God, uncovers resistances to growth, helps catch the scent of the Spirit and encourages the life of prayer—all with a view to leading us to a deeper relationship with Christ and greater fruitfulness in kingdom service.

"A spiritual director is not a counselor, a therapist, or an analyst, but a mature fellow Christian to whom we choose to be accountable for our spiritual life and from whom we can expect prayerful guidance in our constant struggle to discern God's active presence in our lives."

HENRI NOUWEN

An East African proverb relates that antelopes of the African plains travel in herds in order to blow the dust from each other's eyes. Followers of Jesus likewise need one another to mature and advance on the journey. Without a wise and prayerful soul guide we can easily lose our way on life's winding path.

REACH OUT TO OTHERS

When we feel troubled or abandoned, we naturally tend to become self-focused. Rather than brooding over our troubles and wallowing in self-pity, we should shift attention from ourselves to others and their needs. The Great Commandment to love our neighbor (Lk 10:27) remains important through all the seasons of our lives—the easy times and hard times. We reach out to others with love, following the directive of Peter: "love each other as if your life depended on it. Love makes up for practically anything" (1 Pet 4:8 *The Message*). As we compassionately serve others, God uses us to contribute to their transformation in Christ, and in the process we happily discover that our own spirits are uplifted and enriched. Entering into the experience of others who are hurting, we often discover that our own issues appear far less daunting.

Love of others and love of God are inseparable. As we love a brother or sister in their distress we uniquely experience God's love and grace. A chant from the Taizé community in France titled *Ubi Caritas* conveys this point simply but profoundly: "Where there is kindness and love, there God is." Healing and spiritual growth follows the path not of self-seeking or of self-serving but of self-giving. Until we lovingly offer ourselves to others in their season of need we are unlikely to experience the fullness of divine love. Spiritual director Friedrich von Hügel urged distressed souls to move outward toward others in compassionate social engagement. He wrote, "Christianity taught us to care. Caring is the greatest thing, caring matters most."

"It is possible in suffering to be so busy protecting ourselves, so in-turned, that no angel sent by God for our comfort can penetrate."

JOEL WARNE

TAKE COURAGE, NEVER GIVE UP!

Life's distressing seasons call for fortitude, courage and often sheer grit. We need to muster courage because the evil one never ceases to discourage us. Life's challenging trials require that we cling to Jesus and cast off despair. God calls us to be valiant in the face of trials, even as saints in former days were urged to persevere in their hardships. We must courageously endure under every circumstance, confident that in his time and way God will meet us and supply the strength to go on. Puritan pastor Jeremiah Burroughs encouraged disheartened members of his flock to persevere with unwavering faith: "Keep to the path where you were wont [desired] to meet with God, for you shall meet with Him again."

We take courage because of who God is and the incomparable treasure he has stored up for us. Even though sorely harassed and troubled, the apostle Paul acknowledged that "our light and mo-

"Courage faces fear and thereby masters it. Cowardice represses fear and is thereby mastered by it."

MARTIN LUTHER KING JR.

mentary troubles are achieving for us an eternal glory that far outweighs them all" (2 Cor 4:17). It's always too soon for Christians to abandon hope and throw in the towel. The inspired writer of Hebrews urged Christians who were tempted to forsake Christ with these words: "Consider him who endured such opposition from sinners, so that you will not grow weary and lose heart. In your struggle against sin, you have not yet resisted to the point of shedding your blood" (Heb 12:3-4).

Reflect on the following verses from William Cowper, a saint who suffered profoundly on his life's journey.

The saints should never be dismayed,
Nor sink in hopeless fear;
For when they least expect His aid,
The Savior will appear.

Wait for His seasonable aid,
And though it tarry, wait:
The promise may be long delayed,
But cannot come too late.

FOR INDIVIDUAL OR GROUP REFLECTION AND DISCUSSION

1. Ponder thoughtfully Dallas Willard's claim that grace is opposed to earning, not to effort (see p. 105). What insights do you gain into God's gracious working in your life and the necessity of your obedient response to his initiatives?

2. On life's challenging journey, have you intentionally surrendered all to Jesus? Are you steadfastly waiting on him for guid-

ance or deliverance? Are you actively listening to the gentle whispers of the Spirit?

3. How do you rate the quality of your prayer life before God? Have you been encouraged not to give up on God when he appears to delay answers to your prayers?

4. As a result of reading this chapter, when experiencing challenging trials have you been encouraged to trust God and seek him more intentionally?

6   *Joyful Reorientation*

Savor of Resurrection

"LORD, . . .

> *lift me up from the gates of death,*
>
> *that I may declare your praises*
>
> *in the gates of Daughter Zion,*
>
> *and there rejoice in your salvation."*

PSALM 9:13-14

After two decades of service as a missionary and seminary professor I entered a season of confusion brought on by burnout and a stressful midlife transition. I was saying and doing the right things, but my soul became restless and dry. Fortunately I crossed paths with a gifted priest affiliated with the Catholic charismatic movement, and I walked with him for three years in a spiritual mentoring relationship. Under his guidance the pace of my life slowed down, and I practiced neglected spiritual disciplines, read uplifting spiritual classics and processed my dreams.

The spiritual director encouraged me to attend retreats at a Spirit-filled Benedictine monastery in New Mexico. Later, during a sabbatical leave, I enrolled in the community's six-week residential School for Spiritual Direction. The Christlike hospitality of the community, the rhythm of the daily disciplines, inspiring teaching and refreshing hikes with others in the Sangre de Cristo mountains revitalized my soul. The twice-weekly formation groups and individual spiritual direction sessions particularly restored and refreshed me.

As we worshiped, learned, shared and prayed together, I sensed the Spirit bearing me up on the Mount of Transfiguration to behold the glorified Christ, as did Peter, James and John millennia ago. I also sensed that I was being drawn back into the life of the first-century church with its vision, passion and power. Returning home to share these graces with my seminary community, an administrator pulled me aside and said, "You're the most transformed person on this campus." God had accomplished a grace-filled work of revitalizing my soul. My experience mirrored that of the psalmist: "You, GOD, gently and powerfully / put me back on my feet" (Ps 86:17 *The Message*).

God delights in seeing his children move on from the darkness of painful disorientation to the light of joyful reorientation. David experienced pure joy as he was reconciled to God following his sins of adultery and murder.

> Oh, give me back my joy again;
>   you have broken me—
>   now let me rejoice. . . .
> Restore to me the joy of your salvation,
>   and make me willing to obey you. (Ps 51:8, 12 NLT)

Some Christians, unfortunately, fail to make it through seasons of disorientation to experience the delight of joyful reorientation. John of the Cross observed that since many are unwilling to take up Christ's cross, few go the distance. Those, however, who by God's grace do journey all the way through the dark night can anticipate the following surprising outcomes.

FRESH ILLUMINATION

God's command "Let there be light" (Gen 1:3) announced formation of the vast cosmos. The God who called forth light from darkness at the creation also illumines the darkened soul in spiritual reorientation. Hear Isaiah on the fruit of repentance and reorientation: "Arise, shine, for your light has come, / and the glory of the LORD rises upon you" (Is 60:1). God scatters the clouds and illumines the soul's shadows with new light. David exulted, "You light a lamp for me. / The LORD, my God, lights up my darkness" (Ps 18:28 NLT). Saints graced with fresh illumination possess a renewing sense of God's presence and perceive spiritual realities more clearly.

> "God knows exactly how much pressure each one of us can take. He knows how long we can endure the night, so He gives the soul relief, first by welcome glimpses of the morning star and then by the fuller light that harbingers the morning."
>
> A. W. TOZER

John of the Cross described the soul's reorientation paradoxically as the darkness of illumination, whereby God gradually drives away the night with the dawning of a fresh revelation of his love. John illustrated the Spirit's illuminating work in the reoriented soul by comparing it to a log set on fire, its wood drying as flames flare upward. John also likened the soul to a window that permits the light of God to shine through with intense luminosity.

Puritan divines likewise testified to the grace of fresh illumination. One Puritan wrote, "By the goodness of the Lord, the mist is broke up, the clouds are scattered, the face of God appears again, and I find joy and peace and comfort in my soul: yea, the beams of God's favour shine brighter, and the streams of consolation run on more fresh and freely than ever they did." As the storm clouds lift, renewed souls walk in the light of God's presence in a blessed foretaste of heaven's glory.

I have noted that the grief caused by the death of his wife, Joy, thrust C. S. Lewis into a dark pit where he seriously questioned God's goodness. But when he woke up one morning the darkness dissipated and God's face reappeared. "It came this morning early. For various reasons . . . my heart was lighter than it had been for many weeks. . . . After ten days of long-hung grey skies and motionless warm dampness, the sun was shining and there was a light breeze." God graciously brought the distraught apologist back into the light of his presence. Lewis reflected, "I have gradually been coming to feel that the door is no longer shut and bolted. Was it my own frantic need that slammed it in my face?" The distressing crisis left Lewis humbled, with a deeper trust in God.

RADIANCE OF RESURRECTION

If we share in Christ's death through the darkness, then as we come out of it, we also participate in his mighty resurrection. The psalmist expressed this precious hope in these words:

> Though you have made me see troubles,
>   many and bitter,
>   you will restore my life again;
> from the depths of the earth
>   you will again bring me up. (Ps 71:20)

Resurrection by Spirit-power—anticipated in the Old Testament—comes to fulfillment in the New. Eugene Peterson notes:

We live the Christian life out of a rich tradition of formation-by-resurrection. Jesus' resurrection provides the energy and conditions by which we "walk before the Lord in the land of the living" (Ps 116:9). The resurrection of Jesus makes available the reality in which we are formed as new creatures in Christ by the Holy Spirit.

When we emerge from painful disorientation, our life is changed forever. Spiritually, disciples get caught up into Christ's powerful resurrection life and the intellect, will, emotion, moral discrimination and relational capacity all come alive with new energy. Brokenness gives way to wholeness, weakness to strength and bondage to freedom. As God raises us up the power of the old nature comes to an end. The heart is circumcised (see Deut 30:6) and the old self—the former way of defining and experiencing oneself—dies, and the new self in Christ is reborn. Teresa of Ávila illustrated reorientation with the analogy of a silkworm that builds a cocoon, dies in the darkness thereof and emerges as a beautiful butterfly that flutters off in freedom.

"In all of our lives, as in the life of Jesus, the Resurrection has to come, the joy of Easter has to dawn."

Mother Teresa

The reoriented heart hungers for holiness—a life set apart for and empowered by God. A Barna Group update titled "The Concept of Holiness Baffles Most Americans" indicates that only 46 percent "of the born again public believes that God has called them to holiness." Moreover, "young adults (39 or younger) are less likely than middle-aged and older adults to believe that God expects holiness of His people." Findings such as these indicate that many Christians neither understand holiness nor intentionally pursue it. Radically reoriented souls, however, possess a burning passion for holiness in thought, word and deed. Renewed hearts beat with desire to be wholly sanctified. The life of Simon Peter shows the radiance of spiritual resurrection. When Jesus interacted with Simon and six other disciples by the Sea of Galilee (Jn 21), he accomplished a deep work of restoration and transformation. Breakfast on the beach was a soul-searching experience for the defeated disciple. The fire reminded Simon of the fire in the courtyard where he denied his Lord, and he felt again the pain of his three denials. On the beach, Simon, the crusty fisherman, died spiritually and Peter, the "rock," was resurrected. Peter warmly embraced Jesus' forgiving and transforming grace—the grace of joyful reorientation.

The fourteenth-century spiritual writer Julian of Norwich also experienced a spiritual resurrection. After recovering from a life-threatening illness Julian received sixteen "showings" (visions of divine disclosure) followed by a dramatic healing. Her intense sufferings led her to a deeper life of prayer and a more profound awakening to God's love. After her healing Julian wrote, "God allows us to fall; and in his blessed love we are preserved by his strength and wisdom; and through mercy and grace we are raised to a greater abundance of joys." Julian's miraculous restoration inspired her to write that "sin is necessary, but all will be well, and all will be well, and every kind of thing will be well."

INTIMATE UNION

The "in Christ" language of the New Testament reflects another magnificent truth: as believers, we are in union with Christ. From God's perspective we *are* united with Christ when we are born again, but through the grace of surprising reorientation we can *experience* this union more powerfully. Illustrations of this union include Jesus' imagery of the vine and branches (Jn 15:1-8) and the emotional, physical and spiritual union of a husband and a wife within the bond of marriage (Eph 5:28-32).

"Thou being married to him who is God, in him art also one with God. . . . And being thus united and married to him, his spirit flows into thy spirit, and the sap of the Deity sheds itself into thy soul."

FRANCIS ROUS

Paul captures the essence of our mystical union with Christ: "But whoever is united with the Lord is one with him in spirit" (1 Cor 6:17). Reoriented disciples become one with Christ in his mystical body and thus share in the relational community of love among the Father, Son and Holy Spirit. United with the Savior, disciples think with the mind of Christ, form intentions consistent with the will of Christ, feel with the emotions of Christ and conduct themselves following the example of Christ. This grace of reorientation coincides with the so-called Unitive Way of classical Christian spirituality, where God raises Christians above the world system to live in unbroken awareness of his presence.

The grace of reorientation brings greater intimacy with Christ; Christians are spiritually connected to God and feel profoundly known, fully accepted and unconditionally loved. Fleeing to the safety of the desert, David expressed his deep longing for this kind of intimacy:

> You, God, are my God,
>   earnestly I seek you;
> I thirst for you,
>   my whole being longs for you,
> in a dry and parched land
>   where there is no water. (Ps 63:1)

Quietness, attentiveness and communion characterize this union; the bride is content simply to be with the Bridegroom in a loving, contemplative presence. Christian spirituality described this intimate relation as marriage to the heavenly Lover, which John of the Cross said involves "a total transformation in the Beloved."

Intimate union may yield moments of ecstasy—a state of spiritual elation where believers revel in God's love. Peter, James and John caught a glimpse of Jesus transfigured in heavenly glory (Mt 17:2)—an experience that changed them forever. Jesus' face radiated like the sun, and his clothing glistened white like lightening. Moses and Elijah appeared from heaven and spoke with Jesus about his forthcoming death and resurrection. A bright cloud enveloped the disciples, and from it the Father spoke, "This is my Son, whom I love; with him I am well pleased. Listen to him!" (Mt 17:5). The disciples fell prostrate on their faces, overwhelmed with glory from another world. In a hymn Charles Wesley described ecstasy as an appropriate response to the unveiling of God's glory to the soul.

Show me that happiest place,
The place of Thy people's abode,
Where saints in an ecstasy gaze,
And hang on a crucified God.

While disciples should not actively seek experiences of spiritual highs, if God chooses to give them, we can gratefully accept and seek to please him in all areas of our lives.

The Eastern church spoke of union in terms of divinization, or *theosis*, meaning participation in the divine life that makes believers more like Christ. Theologians found support for divinization in Scriptures such as 2 Peter 1:4, which states that through Christ's

"What is a divinized or a sanctified person? . . . The person who transmits and radiates the eternal and divine Light and burns with divine love, that person is sanctified or divinized."

THE THEOLOGIA GERMANICA

promises believers "participate in the divine nature." Western
Christians understand divinization to mean that saints share in
the life of God through the energy of the Spirit in a spiritual union,
without fusing the human and the divine. The term *divinization*
appears frequently in *The Theologia Germanica* as a near synonym
for sanctification. Divinization finds expression in another hymn
of Charles Wesley.

> He deigns in flesh to appear,
> Widest extremes to join;
> To bring our vileness near,
> And make us all divine:
> And we the life of God shall know,
> For God is manifested below.

To sum up, Brennan Manning asserts, "The deepest desire of
our hearts is for union with God. From the first moment of our
existence our most powerful yearn-
ing is to fulfill the original purpose
of our lives—'to see Him more
clearly, love Him more dearly, follow
Him more nearly.' " He adds, "We are
made for God, and nothing else will
satisfy."

"We will never become

absorbed into God, but are

united with His loving will.

This is what 'deification'

means."

BERNARD OF CLAIRVAUX

NEW HEALING

Spirit reorientation also heals emotional wounds and other issues that
impede transformation in Christ. Because the human person is a
unity of soul/spirit and body, spiritual problems cannot be isolated from psychological problems. We humans suffer emotional
and relational shortfalls that impede spiritual growth. But through
the grace of reorientation the deep roots of bitterness, feelings of
inferiority or superiority, areas of mistrust and painful memories

are graced with new healing. Destructive works of the flesh yield to the life-giving fruit of the Spirit (Gal 5:19-24).

Moreover, we joyfully exchange pride for humility, anxiety for peace, fright for reverential fear, despair for hope and worthlessness for the assurance of being valued and loved. Men strengthen underdeveloped feminine qualities, particularly intuition, empathy, vulnerability and relationality. Women strengthen underdeveloped masculine qualities, such as strength, courage and assertiveness. Both men and women realize a greater integration of feminine and masculine after the pattern of Jesus himself.

"Healing is for us today. Whatever God did and was able to do and willing to do at any time, God is able and willing to do again, within the framework of His will."

A. W. TOZER

As we resolve these spiritual and emotional deficits, we gain a new sense of wholeness. We now live not in the head alone but out of the richness of the heart. The Spirit frees us from compulsive behavior patterns, enslaving addictions and vulnerability to satanic deception, and we are better able to obey and honor God under all circumstances. As summed up by Paul, "Christ has set us free to live a free life. . . . Never again let anyone put a harness of slavery on you" (Gal 5:1 *The Message*).

Reoriented believers also experience the divine shalom—the blessing of peace Jesus gave to his faithful followers. Paul confidently exclaimed, "The peace of God, which transcends all understanding, will guard your hearts and your minds in Christ Jesus" (Phil 4:7). According to Puritan Joseph Symonds, "You have a right to peace and comfort, for it is that which Christ died for, and which he hath left as a legacy to his people."

The risen Christ brought Simon Peter deep, inner healing and integration in his spiritual reorientation. Formerly strong-willed and opinionated, Peter developed integrity in his inward self. Formerly impulsive, he became self-controlled. Formerly unstable, Peter was made strong and steady. Formerly captivated by religious phenomena, Peter was grateful for, but not fixed on, powerful spiritual experiences. Formerly fearful of others' power over him, Peter now had confident strength ruling his heart. No longer ashamed of Christ, reoriented Peter boldly and courageously testified to the Savior, confessing him Lord of all (1 Pet 3:15).

Reorientation brings inner healing that shatters our old patterns in favor of a new reality—restoration of the image of God in us. This healing facilitates the flowering of our true self as God intended it to be. Spiritual, emotional and physical healing enables us to live as dynamic disciples, empowered to serve God's high kingdom purposes. The Hebrew prophet eagerly anticipated this holistic rejuvenation: "For you who revere my name, the sun of righteousness will rise with healing in its rays" (Mal 4:2).

WISDOM

We also gain wisdom as another grace of the reoriented life. Many modern cultures are obsessed with information and knowledge—abundantly accessible thanks to digital technology (the Internet at this writing contains well over a billion sites). However, those who gather vast knowledge are not necessarily wise, for wisdom issues in God-honoring choices and righteous living. Wisdom is a rich gift of God (Jas 1:5-7) that invites cultivation on our part.

Solomon asked God for wisdom that he might rule his domain well (1 Kings 3:7-12). God honored Solomon's request and endowed the king with "a wise and discerning heart" (1 Kings 3:12) that equipped him for many noble accomplishments. Solomon testified, "The Lord gives wisdom," adding:

Then you will understand what is right and just
    and fair—every good path.

For wisdom will enter your heart,
and knowledge will be pleasant to your soul.
(Prov 2:6, 9-10)

The entire book of Proverbs addresses the virtue of wisdom. Wisdom is intensely practical. People of wisdom honor their parents, speak judiciously, labor diligently and treat subordinates fairly. They handle money prudently, give generously to the needy and flee immorality. In a crowded world of diminishing resources, wise folks leave a small carbon footprint (pollution) embedded on the earth. Wise people honor God with their whole lives—hence the link between wisdom and fear of the Lord (Prov 9:10). Ultimately, wisdom is centered in Jesus Christ—"the power of God and the wisdom of God" (1 Cor 1:24). The truly wise person understands that Christ infinitely overshadows every earthly reality.

A friend whom I will call Josh graduated from a prestigious university with an engineering degree and an M.B.A. His father, who owns a business with international operations, groomed his son to assume leadership in the company. Josh soon found himself supervising the company's international operations with frequent travel. Initially, the rush of expanding the business proved invigorating. But after a few years Josh realized that his work left him with little time and energy for family and nurturing his relationship with God. After prayerful reflection, Josh concluded that he must adjust his lifestyle to be more consistent with eternal values. Josh took a lower-level job in the company that allowed more time for family, his local church, spiritual pursuits and recreation. Josh exchanged prestige for practical wisdom.

Discernment, understanding and sound judgment are siblings of wisdom (see Prov 2:1-6). Reoriented disciples have greater insight into life and deeper understanding of spiritual realities. Blessed with the mind of Christ, "the person with the Spirit makes judgments about all things" (1 Cor 2:15). Discerning people look

behind newspaper headlines and opinion polls to perceive the
true state of affairs. Reflecting on worldwide crises, they understand that there are no political solutions to spiritual problems.
Believers gifted with insight point to a more faithful way forward
spiritually, socially, politically and economically. Wise and discerning disciples understand that life embraces many shades of
gray, and they respect the complexities, ambiguities and para-
doxes of life.

BECOMING A CHILD AGAIN

A leading sign of spiritual maturity in Scripture is childlikeness.
Our Lord himself identified this as a key quality of the spiritually
reoriented person. Consistently using the Greek word *paidion* (a
child up to age seven), our Lord taught the following on this
theme:

- "Truly I tell you, unless you change and become like little children, you will never enter the kingdom of heaven. Therefore,
  whoever takes a humble place—becoming like this child—is
  the greatest in the kingdom of heaven. And whoever welcomes
  one such child in my name welcomes me" (Mt 18:3-5).

- "Let the little children come to me, and do not hinder them, for
  the kingdom of God belongs to such as these. Truly I tell you,
  anyone who will not receive the kingdom of God like a little
  child will never enter it" (Mk 10:14-15).

What did Jesus mean by becoming a child? What values did he
commend in the little ones he held up as a standard of righteousness? What qualities might Jesus have had in mind when he urged
people to become like little children? Consider the following
possibilities:

- A child delights to be held and loved by a trusted caregiver.
  Spiritual writer Thérèse of Lisieux fashioned her "little Way"
  after the pattern of children at play. She portrayed spirituality

as a relationship with God in which we are like small children who are not driven by achievement but simply by dependence on God.

- A child naturally trusts worthy caregivers. Complete confidence in God, who is loving, wise and good, is a bedrock quality of Christian maturity. Spiritually mature people implicitly trust God and his purposes, thereby overcoming fear and anxiety in an uncertain world.

- A child is lighthearted and spontaneous. A small child displays a spur-of-the-moment excitement at being alive. At heart a child is cheerful rather than somber, delighting in laugh and play. Spiritually reoriented people likewise possess a zest for life that arises from the deepest recesses of the heart.

- A child asks honest but profound questions that more inhibited adults might not think of posing. Before blessing the family meal one evening, our daughter, Sharon, announced, "Let's talk to God and give thanks for our food." Whereupon three-year-old Sophie with refreshing candor asked, "Where is God?" (She now knows that God is everywhere.)

- A child embodies lack of premeditation and relative innocence. Paul had this quality in mind when he wrote, "In regard to evil be infants" (1 Cor 14:20). The hearts of mature saints are oriented not toward evil designs and actions but toward truth, kindness and justice.

- A child enjoys the simple things of life and possesses a fertile imagination. For a child, mystery is not a problem to be solved but a wonder to be enjoyed. Through the genre of imaginative fiction, writers such as C. S. Lewis kindle childlike wonder in their readers.

However counterintuitive it might appear, the quality of childlikeness constitutes "a paradoxical ideal of maturity."

JOURNEY OUTWARD

God never wants his children to be entirely focused on themselves. The compassionate One permits his children to experience suffering in order to be empowered to serve others. Grace that remains undispensed becomes stale. In the divine economy disciples who have experienced a transforming inner journey are propelled outward by the Spirit in compassionate service to others. If we are properly exercised and responsive, an outward journey of service inevitably follows an inward journey of renewal. So the psalmist testified, "I've made Lord GOD my home. / GOD, I'm telling the world what you do!" (Ps 73:28 *The Message*).

Theologian Robert E. Webber wrote about "the journey inward into the mystery of God within and the journey outward into the mystery of other people." No one has to twist the arm of spiritually reoriented saints to get them to journey outward in selfless service to others. We who have been healed and repatterned serve with fresh purpose so that others might enter the circle of blessing. Having been deeply graced in the core of our beings, we tell the good news of new life in Jesus. Our Lord himself is our model for this others-centered phase of life's journey: "For even the Son of Man did not come to be served, but to serve, and to give his life as a ransom for many" (Mk 10:45).

Many biblical people pursued outward journeys of service following seasons of distress and darkness. After passing through a painful season of disobedience, Jonah finally obeyed God by preaching to the people of Nineveh. Simon Peter, after his denial of Jesus and subsequent restoration, was redirected outward, assuming leadership in the early Jewish-Christian church. We see a similar inward-outward pattern in the life of Paul. Following his dramatic conversion, Paul sojourned for two-and-a-half years in the desert on an extended inner journey. After coming to understand the gospel better and deepening his relationship with Christ,

Paul was propelled outward by the Spirit to the Gentile world as Christendom's greatest missionary.

A false form of mysticism called *quietism*, which rejected outer journeys of service and mission, arose in the seventeenth century under the influence of (among others) Jeanne Guyon. As the name suggests, this impulse emphasized quietness of soul. Quietists believed that no effort was necessary to respond to the promptings of grace, resist temptation or acquire virtue. Inviting resignation to our sinful condition and apathy toward the neighbor, quietism was a poor paradigm of the life of discipleship. Contemplation and action—together— form an authentic pattern of the reoriented life in Christ. A redemptive journey of personal and community formation and a mission journey on behalf of others must advance in tandem.

> "Renewal cannot come to the church unless its people are on an outward journey."
>
> ELIZABETH O'CONNOR

Return for a moment to my life-giving sojourn in the renewal community that I mentioned earlier (see p. 127). I was assigned to a spiritual formation group with five others. As we openly shared our lives with one another, God bonded us together at a deep spiritual level. As our final meeting was drawing to a close with prayer, Jesus through the Spirit astonishingly stood in the midst of the circle and spoke directly to my heart, saying, "Bruce, these weeks have been a life-transforming journey for you. Having been healed and renewed, I ask you to surrender your life in service to others. Along the pathway of your life I want you to lay down footprints of blessing others." In that sacred moment I responded, "Lord, this is wonderful. But if I should forget myself and sacrifice my life in love for others, who will care for me?" Jesus immediately replied with the reassuring words, "I will!" The restorative inward journey leads—as it always does by God's grace—to an outward journey of service to others.

LIVING IN LOVE

The Spirit faithfully impels reoriented believers into a life of others-centered love. Whereas earlier on the journey we were often self-focused, we now become others-focused because we've been reoriented and transformed. With egocentricity uprooted by God's discipline, our capacity to love others is enlarged. The love in view is primarily a decision of the will rather than an emotion. It is a choice to set aside self-interest for the enrichment of others. Gerald May noted that "contemplatives of all traditions agree on one certain thing— the spiritual life is all about love." Thus, he says, "the dark night of the soul exists for the sole purpose of furthering love."

"The more a person loves,

the closer he approaches

the image of God."

MARTIN LUTHER

Classical Greek has four principal words for love. *Philia* denotes friendship, *storgē* affection within the family circle and *eros* sensual love. Our concern is with the fourth word, *agapē*, meaning self-giving love. Joseph Stowell identified four elements of *agapē* love: Not primarily a feeling or an emotion, *agapē* involves a choice, a willful decision and commitment. Second, *agapē* possesses a distinctive focus on others in which lovers are devoted to and sacrifice for the object of their love. Next, *agapē* possesses a discernible "feltness"; in other words, it does engage our emotions and affections. Finally, *agapē* blesses others and lifts them up.

A first fruit of spiritual transformation is the ravishing delight of being loved by God. Reoriented saints breathe in God's no-strings-attached love just as we take in air. We soon discover that being loved by God is all that we want or need in life. Luxuriating in God's ravishing love expels fear and anxiety from our hearts: "There is no fear in love. But perfect love drives out fear, because fear has to do with punishment. The one who fears is not made perfect in love"

(1 Jn 4:18). Awareness of God's love frees us from false dependencies, our need for approval from others and much more.

Reoriented disciples in return love God. "Though you have not seen him, you love him . . . and are filled with an inexpressible and glorious joy, for you are receiving the end result of your faith, the salvation of your souls" (1 Pet 1:8-9). As reoriented disciples we serve God not out of obligation or for reward, but out of sheer love for him. Transformed saints joyfully fulfill the Great Commandment: "Hear, O Israel: The LORD our God, the LORD is one. Love the LORD your God with all your heart and with all your soul and with all your strength" (Deut 6:4-5). The almighty God delights immensely in the love we bring to him.

Following the death of his beloved son Adeodatus ("given by God"), Augustine experienced the power of renewed love. Whereas despair once ruled the great theologian's heart, love for God now consumed him. Reflecting on his convoluted journey from philosophy to belief in God to Christ, Augustine wrote odes of love to God, such as the following:

- "I love you alone, Lord. I seek You alone. I yearn to be possessed by You alone."

- "O Lord, I love you. I love, I burn, I pant for You. I trample under foot all that gives here delight. I want to go to you."

So great was Thérèse of Lisieux's devotion to Christ she determined that her vocation would simply be love. Following this path of love she offered the following testimonies:

- "Since that day, I have been soaked and engulfed in love."

- "All is fleeting that we cherish here under the sun. The only good thing is to love God with all one's heart and to remain poor in spirit."

The Christian's greatest privilege on earth and in heaven is to love God and delight in him. Through this exchange of love, we are enabled to love other people without condition. In Scripture, love for God and love for others are joined at the hip. God's love cherished in the heart impels love for others. As the apostle John put it, "We love because he first loved us" (1 Jn 4:19), and "Anyone who does not love remains in death" (1 Jn 3:14). Jesus commanded his followers to love, adding "Love your neighbor as yourself" (Mk 12:31) to the original Hebrew Shema, the command to love God with our whole being. Love cares for its object by sharing material provisions and nurturing spiritual life.

"Love has hands to love others.

It has feet to hasten to the

poor and needy. It has eyes to

see misery and want. It has ears

to hear the sighs and sorrows

of men. This is what love

looks like."

AUGUSTINE

Paul's language in Romans shows a heart consumed with love for his unsaved friends: "I have great sorrow and unceasing anguish in my heart. For I could wish that I myself were cursed and cut off from Christ for the sake of my people, those of my own race, the people of Israel" (Rom 9:2-4). Other-directed love embraces brothers and sisters in Christ with particular affection. Jesus placed this high obligation on us with the injunction, "A new command I give you: Love one another. As I have loved you, so you must love one another. By this everyone will know that you are my disciples, if you love one another" (Jn 13:34-35). Peter replicated this command of Jesus: "Now that you have purified yourselves by obeying the truth so that you have sincere love for each other, love one another deeply, from the heart" (1 Pet 1:22).

Love for God and others becomes our defining virtue as friends of Jesus. The children of God and the offspring of the devil are distinguished not by the greatness of their accomplishments but by their love. Reoriented Christians pursue the *summum bonum* (the greatest good) of the kingdom: Christlike living in sacrificial love, even toward those whom we dislike or who may have injured us. John of the Cross noted that because there is nothing greater than love, we will be judged on the extent to which we have loved well. "When evening comes, you will be examined in love. Learn to love as God desires to be loved and abandon your own ways of acting." As apprentices of the Lamb we do well to ask, *Am I more loving now than earlier on my journey?*

> *"Love is superior to everything: sweeter than anything, more courageous than anything, higher than anything, wider than anything, more pleasing than anything, more fulfilling than anything, better than anything in heaven or earth."*
>
> THOMAS À KEMPIS

CONTEMPLATE ETERNAL REALITIES

Although the glory of Christ shines on us here below, we look beyond the present to the glory of the everlasting kingdom—a glory that exceeds the splendor enjoyed by Adam and Eve in the Garden. As Paul put it, "For our light and momentary troubles are achieving for us an eternal glory that far outweighs them all. So we fix our eyes not on what is seen, but on what is unseen, since what is seen is temporary, but what is unseen is eternal" (2 Cor 4:17-18). Saints meditate on the church's prayer that "Thine is the kingdom, and the power and the glory forever."

Calvin observed that the Christian life involves three essential acts: self-denial, cross-bearing and meditation on the delights of heaven. No longer dazzled by the lights of this world, reoriented disciples direct their minds toward heaven and meditate on its unfading splendor. Contemplation of heaven reveals the fleeting nature of this life, refocuses the soul on what is eternal and deepens devotion to the glorified Lord. We meditate on the future life

"For here we do not have an enduring city, but we are looking for the city that is to come."

HEBREWS 13:14

not by emptying our minds but by saturating our minds with the Word of God. Particularly helpful in this venture are relevant Old Testament prophecies, the Sermon on the Mount and the book of Revelation.

Pilgrim saints, moreover, enjoy a foretaste of the endless life that is ours in heaven. God grants us moments of awe and wonder in this life as we think about the wedding of the Lamb and his bride (Rev 19:7, 9). Augustine encouraged this practice of savoring eternity. He wrote, "Give me one who longs, who hungers, who is the thirsty pilgrim in this wilderness, sighing after the springs of his eternal homeland; give me such a one, he will know what I mean." As God grants glimpses of eternity, we store its glory in our hearts to push us onward for the remainder of our earthly journey.

Reoriented Peter, for example, treasured the memory of Christ's glory revealed on the Mount of Transfiguration.

> We were eyewitnesses of his majesty. He received honor and glory from God the Father when the voice came to him from the Majestic Glory, saying, "This is my Son, whom I love; with him I am well pleased." We ourselves heard this voice that came from heaven when we were with him on the sacred mountain. (2 Pet 1:16-18)

The memory of this awesome event strengthened Peter for the rigors of apostolic ministry.

Fashioned for another world, reoriented believers long to be with Christ in heaven. Richard Baxter was the greatest preacher of the seventeenth century. While serving as chaplain in Cromwell's army, Baxter experienced an illness in 1647 in which he lost two quarts of blood. He spent five months recuperating in the home of friends where he read Scripture and contemplated the glories of heaven. Baxter testified that contemplation of heaven (even claiming to hear angel choruses above) kindled his desire to join Christ in his heavenly home. The outcomes of Baxter's meditations on heaven are recorded in *The Saints Everlasting Rest.*

I have outlined in this chapter the main features of our reorientation in Christ, by which all things are made new. Regrettably, we must also acknowledge that not all Christians reach this season of joyful reorientation. Some are not prepared to pay the price of total surrender, rugged trust or perseverance amidst trials. Along the challenging pathway we may fail to accept and respond to the gift of God's enabling grace. John of the Cross explained the failure to experience the joy of reorientation with these words: "The reason is not that God wishes only a few of these spirits to be so elevated; he would rather want all to be perfect, but he finds few vessels that will endure so lofty and sublime a work."

"Trials help us detach ourselves from the earth; they make us look higher than this world. Here below nothing can satisfy us."

THÉRÈSE OF LISIEUX

WE SHALL BE LIKE HIM

The perplexing and joyful journey of spiritual orientation, disorientation and reorientation is nearing its earthly end. Followers of the Lamb anticipate the day when, separated from our lifeless bodies, we enter paradise and meet Jesus. The psalmist anticipated this precious hope of the intermediate heaven: "You guide me with your counsel, / and afterward you will take me into glory" (Ps 73:24). All darkness, pain and tears will be left behind. Having crossed the great divide, we will look on Christ's face, behold him as he is and know that we are home. In the words of Paul, "Now we see only a reflection as in a mirror; then we shall see face to face. Now I know in part; then I shall know fully, even as I am fully known" (1 Cor 13:12). For the first time, we will see our indescribable God as he truly is.

When Christ returns to earth at the end of the age the bodies of deceased and living believers will be raised, reunited with our undying souls/spirits and changed to be like Christ's glorious body (1 Cor 15:35-49). Redeemed humanity finally will be liberated from the ravages of sin and conformed to the image of God's Son. With this reunion of souls/spirits with transformed bodies, our final destiny will be realized in the New Jerusalem. All who have suffered for Christ will be glorified with him.

"After many transformations, perfected, your souls will receive wings to fly up to heaven, having sown on earth the fertile seed of their state of self-surrender to live in others for ever."

JEAN PIERRE DE CAUSSADE

Hügel noted that "if we are Christians there are always two notes, suffering and joy. Gethsemane is awful, but it does not end with Gethsemane; there is the Resurrection." Because resurrection follows death, "Christianity is so balanced."

Life in heaven will involve an unveiling of the glory of the triune God, in which we will enjoy eternity with the Father, Son and Spirit in unbroken communion of love and praise. We will be joyfully reunited with believing loved ones who have gone before, and will relish fellowship with distinguished saints of old: with Abraham, Moses, Isaiah, and with Jesus' disciples and apostles. Humble believers will embrace Augustine, Luther, Wesley, Mother Teresa and countless others who lived courageous lives for Christ. We will learn firsthand of their love, sacrifice, perseverance and in some cases martyrdom. All God's people will be graced with joy and rewarding service throughout eternity.

FOR INDIVIDUAL OR GROUP REFLECTION
AND DISCUSSION

1. If you have transitioned from darkness into light—from the wintertime of the soul to the warmth of summer—what was this experience like for you? If you are still in a season of disequilibrium or darkness, how has this chapter encouraged your heart?

2. Prayerfully reflect on the profound moral and spiritual union that is our heritage in Christ as taught in Scripture. What specific steps might you take to deepen union and communion with the Savior?

3. Ponder the paradox that the more we are transformed by grace into the likeness of Christ, the more we become aware of our uncleanness in the brilliance of God's holiness (see Is 6:1-5).

7   *Conclusion*

"You're blessed when you stay on course,

*walking steadily on the road revealed by G*OD.

You're blessed when you follow his directions,

doing your best to find him."

PSALM 119:1-2 *The Message*

I will now briefly sum up the shape of the spiritual journey we have considered in our study thus far.

OUR APPOINTED GOAL

God created all people with a desire (however repressed) to know him and to be owned by him. This deep human longing is satisfied not by any created thing but as we are swept up by faith into the grace and love of the trinitarian life. Only then will our restless hearts be fulfilled. Only then will we love, glorify and serve God—the purposes for which we were created and redeemed.

I have portrayed the Christian life as a challenging journey through the wilderness of this world to our eternal home in heaven. The goal of the journey is that by God's grace we might be presented "fully mature in Christ" (Col 1:28). As noted earlier, the word *mature* indicates wholeness or completeness of heart. Our goal as believers is to live the full life God intended for us. As Paul put it, God's purpose is that "we all reach unity in the faith and in the knowledge of the Son of God and become mature, attaining to the whole measure of the fullness of Christ" (Eph 4:13). What is this but the realization of Jesus' command in the Beatitudes to "be perfect . . . as your heavenly Father is perfect" (Mt 5:48). The wholeness or maturity God intends for us consists in growing conformity to his Son, Jesus (1 Jn 3:2).

JESUS OUR COURSE

Our course on the journey, as Augustine pointed out, is the person of Jesus Christ himself. "Christ as God is the homeland where we are going. Christ as Man is the Way we must travel." Above all, then, we must keep our eyes fixed on him, the pioneer who has paved the way. When mist and clouds obscure our path we will not always have a clear view of what God is up to in our lives. We must, therefore, steadfastly trust him even when life doesn't make sense. Maturity is never achieved quickly; the journey must run its long, winding course. We can facilitate advance on the journey, but we cannot outrun God's timetable.

> "My Lord God . . . I do not see the road ahead of me. . . . Therefore I will trust you always."
>
> THOMAS MERTON

As has been repeatedly observed, on our passage through the seasons of life we encounter both blessings and hardships. The road we travel to the Father's house is graced with favor and mercy, but it is also narrow and at times difficult. Like John Bunyan's

Pilgrim, disciples face many uncertainties and bear many burdens
along the pathway to the Celestial City.

Wisely and lovingly God allows us to experience lows so he
can raise us up to healing heights. He permits us to become pow-
erless on our own so he can empower us in Christ. By the purifying fire of his love he empties us of our lowly self in order to fill
us with his exalted self. The symbol of our faith, after all, is not
a comfortable couch but a rugged cross. The pilgrim journey embraces many puzzling polarities that prompt perplexity and distress. Ponder the following prayer penned by a Puritan divine
from the past:

> Let me learn by paradox
> that the way down is the way up,
> that to be low is to be high,
> that the broken heart is the healed heart,
> that the contrite spirit is the rejoicing spirit,
> that the repenting soul is the victorious soul,
> that to have nothing is to possess all,
> that to bear the cross is to wear the crown,
> that to give is to receive,
> that the valley is the place of vision.

THE INEVITABLE PRESSURE

On the journey disciples will encounter seasons of distress, disorientation and perhaps dark nights. Scripture and Christian spiritual writings attest that Jesus' apprentices must pass through me-
andering trails and scorching flames. Reflecting on painful
personal experiences, David wrote, "I used to wander off until you
disciplined me" (Ps 119:67 NLT). The most beloved of psalms
teaches that only when we "walk through the darkest valley" can
we truly say, "You are close beside me" (Ps 23:4 NLT).

Jesus straightforwardly told his followers, "Here on earth you will have many trials and sorrows" (Jn 16:33 NLT). Like other people, Christians contend with betrayal, emotional struggles and serious physical illnesses. Believers experience "labors and sorrows, temptations and trials, anxieties, weaknesses, necessities, injuries, slanders, rebukes, humiliations, confusions, corrections and contempt." Christians on the journey suffer assaults from Satan and persecution from the unbelieving world. We never seek out pain or tragedy but we are realists, accepting their inevitability in this life. We're not blown out of the water when bad things happen to good people. Our distresses and dark nights are both providential and redemptive, for they purify our lives, draw us closer to God and align us with his perfect will. God wisely turns up the heat of his refiner's fire when he sees gold worth purifying.

God longs to draw us into more intimate relationship with himself.

"If God has singled you out to be a special object of His grace, you may expect Him to honor you with stricter discipline and greater suffering than less favored ones are called upon to endure."

A. W. TOZER

He uses trials for our personal and corporate formation. The perplexity and pain we encounter along the path unmask and reconfigure our souls in Christ. Somewhat sternly, the famous British preacher Charles Spurgeon testified: "I owe everything to the furnace and the hammer. I have made no progress in heavenly things except when I have been whipped by the great Schoolmaster. The best piece of furniture in my house has been the cross."

The Dutch theologian Abraham Kuyper insisted that "prosperity and pleasure *never* bring people closer to God." The reality is that the people God uses greatly in kingdom service he often allows to be wounded. The unsettling seasons we encounter on the journey are necessary both for our transformation in Christ and

for gaining the wisdom to guide others on their homeward journeys. Our greatest need, therefore, is not to avoid distress and
suffering, but to live into the process and patiently permit our
hardships to do their transforming work.

Peter, who crashed and failed under trial, wrote, "Dear friends,
do not be surprised at the fiery ordeal that has come on you to test
you, as though something strange were happening to you. But rejoice
inasmuch as you participate in the sufferings of Christ, so that you may
be overjoyed when his glory is revealed" (1 Pet 4:12-13). Thankfully,
though the Spirit prunes and refines us, he also brings overflowing joy
and hope. The book containing the charges of sin against us has been
nailed to the cross, and Jesus is now our brother, and the Lord of the cosmos our Father. Nothing in all creation can separate us from God's love.
We have been blessed with grace upon grace, and though God's dealings with us may be mysterious, he is never uncaring or unjust, for
he does it all out of love.

"What is troubling you?

Poverty? Ridicule? Failure?

Inward and outward crosses?

Look on all these things as

genuine favors from the hand

of God, distributed to his

friends, favors that he allows

you to share."

François Fénelon

As they begin to understand the purpose of disorienting seasons, some believers—particularly those young in the faith—ask,
"Is it necessary that I pass through unsettling and painful experiences?" Understandably we all seek to avoid physical, emotional
and spiritual suffering. However, the answer to the above question
must be yes—as the previous chapters suggest. In my teaching I
often advise students—especially young ones—to fasten their
seat belts securely, for the journey will likely be bumpy.

Mother Teresa, who spent five decades among the destitute and dying in Calcutta, served in a virtually endless state of "doubt, loneliness, and abandonment [where] God seemed absent, heaven empty, and bitterest of all, her own suffering seemed to count for nothing." Who would doubt that Mother Teresa's fruitfulness stemmed in large measure from her life of suffering?

A REPETITIVE PATTERN

Among the many paradigms that portray the spiritual journey, there is wisdom in Walter Brueggemann's observation that "each of God's children is in transit along the flow of orientation, disorientation, and reorientation." Moving through these major phases of the journey will prove both rewarding and challenging. Our tendency as pain-avoidant humans is to pursue a peaceful balance and accept the comfortable status quo. But as many spiritual masters have taught, those who fail to increase decrease, and those who fail to advance regress. Like a mountain climber pressing on to the steep summit, we must overcome forces that weigh us down and strive for the goal with resolute intention, all the while practicing healthy spiritual habits.

The maturity to which God calls us also requires courage, tenacity and prudent risk-taking as we move into unexplored territory. Above all, we must take up the cross that Jesus bore and tread the path of rejection, suffering and redemption with him. Trusting God, we must endure all that life this side of Eden brings our way. Throwing in the towel of defeat is no option for followers of the all-conquering Christ. Ultimately, the trials we bear prove to be blessings, for in the mystery of providence fragile self-trust gives way to sturdy God-trust and our death-dealing flesh is overcome by the life-giving Spirit.

Given the fluid, dynamic and cyclical nature of the journey, progress inevitably requires revisiting earlier seasons of difficulty and darkness. I repeat the point made earlier that ultimately believers journey through the major phases successively, but we also cycle through these seasons throughout the course of our lives. That we sometimes repeat this learning process is clear in the history of Joseph, who experienced disorientation of major proportions when his brothers sought to kill him. Later, Joseph was promoted to a high position in Potiphar's household, but then falsely accused of making sexual advances at the king's wife and thrown into prison for several years.

Jonah's journey also shows repeated experiences of painful disorientation. He faced desolation in the belly of a great fish and later sank into bitter distress when the Ninevites, whom he despised, repented and welcomed God's favor. Paul, the seasoned apostle, also encountered repeated occasions of distress on his journey—for example, when he agonized intensely over indwelling sin in his life (Rom 7:14-25). In this sense we understand Teresa of Ávila's prudent counsel that "no one becomes so advanced that they don't often have to return to the beginning." Having passed through this process once, however, we should gain priceless wisdom to help us in subsequent seasons of distress.

STEADY PROGRESS

The good news is that although likely to revisit previous phases of the journey, by God's grace we advance toward the goal. But just as recovery from major surgery often occurs slowly, so spiritual progress often is gradual. We shouldn't be discouraged by the slow pace of our upward path. Through all the unexpected changes of the journey God is there to guide, provide and sustain us. We never travel alone, for Jesus himself and fellow believers travel alongside us. We are encouraged by the "great cloud of witnesses" (Heb

"Darkness is not driven away immediately. Light comes in small increments, moment by moment. . . . Purging the soul is a lifetime effort."

FRANCIS OF SALES

12:1)—men and women of faith who have gone before and mapped out the landscape for us.

As we journey we recognize that the goal is never quite reached in this life. Here below we sacrifice and strive, but moral and spiritual perfection is never fully attained. As Adrian van Kaam put it, "We're only on the road toward likeness with the sacrificial life of Jesus. We never arrive; we are always arriving."

Young disciples can be encouraged because spiritual maturity and godliness are not beyond their reach. Ponder the path of Thérèse of Lisieux, who suffered physically and spiritually for twenty-four short years, but who in dedicating her young life to Jesus achieved profound intimacy with the Savior. Although perfection is unattainable in this life, we nevertheless strive toward the goal of imaging Jesus Christ, who alone is "the way and the truth and the life" (Jn 14:6).

JOYFUL ARRIVAL

Our pop-psychology culture stresses process rather than goal. Biblical faith, however, emphasizes the importance of both the journey process (and the need to embrace it for the sake of transformation) as well as its glorious end or goal. Jesus Christ is both our homeward course and our heavenly destination, and our God has made provisions to ensure that we meet him at the road's end no matter what challenges we face on our journey. We who love Jesus may move securely through the challenging seasons of our lives, encouraged by knowing our final end. We experience blessed transformation of spirit and life in measure here below, but we will be radically renewed throughout the rolling ages of eternity in the presence of God, his angels and the vast company of the redeemed.

> "God will be all in all and will be wonderful in His saints, and we shall be altogether pure and new creatures of His."
>
> MARTIN LUTHER

The Savior who went before us on the journey and arrived at his appointed destination promises us unspeakable bliss in the life to come. Faithful elders gathered around the heavenly throne herald the destiny of God's triumphant people in these stirring words:

> They are before the throne of God
>   and serve him day and night in his temple;
> and he who sits on the throne
>   will spread his tent over them.
> "Never again will they hunger;
>   never again will they thirst.
> The sun will not beat down on them,"
>   nor any scorching heat.
> For the Lamb at the center before the throne
>   will be their shepherd;
> "he will lead them to springs of living water."
>   "And God will wipe away every tear from their eyes."
> (Rev 7:15-17)

As we journey toward heaven we should consider the advice of the writer of Hebrews: "let us throw off everything that hinders and the sin that so easily entangles. And let us run with perseverance the race marked out for us, fixing our eyes on Jesus, the pioneer and perfecter of faith" (Heb 12:1-2). The conclusion of our journey is beyond all human comprehension: We will see God face to face! We will become like Jesus! We will be with the Father, the Son and the Spirit forever, luxuriating in immeasurable mercy, love and grace. In our heavenly home prepared by the Father there will be no sorrow, no pain, no perplexity, no struggle with evil and no night. Arriving at our journey's destination we will discover that everything has been made gloriously and eternally new in Christ (Rom 8:20-21).

FOR INDIVIDUAL OR GROUP REFLECTION AND DISCUSSION

1. Reflecting on your own spiritual journey, are you able to identify seasons you have thus far traveled through? Describe these phases in your own words. In what major season of the soul do you find yourself at present?

2. What forces (physical, emotional or spiritual) presently seem to be slowing your progress to greater maturity and satisfaction in Christ? Name them as best you can.

3. Think about relevant Scriptures and Christian writings that portray the glory that awaits us in heaven. How does contemplation of the glory of the life to come encourage your heart and keep you dedicated to the kingdom here and now?

4. How might our reflection on major seasons of the spiritual journey enable you to minister spiritual guidance more effectively to others on their challenging life paths?

Appendix

Spiritual Journey Paradigms:
Classical and Contemporary

Christian thinkers throughout history have proposed various paradigms or examples of the spiritual journey. I encourage readers who are interested in more detailed portraits of the spiritual journey to study some of these paradigms, outlined here. The journeys described by leading spiritual authorities are like a sparkling diamond with many facets. Since each journey paradigm often focuses on one facet of the diamond (e.g., love, prayer), it affords a partial representation of the richness and complexity of our growing life in Christ. We gain a more holistic understanding of the soul's journey to maturity by reflecting on several paradigms in their richness and diversity.

THE "TRIPLE WAY"
Patristic and medieval authorities developed the "Triple Way" paradigm for the spiritual journey that progresses from purgation to illumination to union with God. First, the way of purgation

comprises conversion to Christ, purification of sins and self-denial by the practice of spiritual disciplines, including prayer and loosening attachment to material things. Transition to the next stage often involves the dark night of the senses.

Second, the way of illumination involves yielding to the light and grace of the Spirit, deepening love for God and others, and developing virtues such as humility, self-control, patience and generosity. Here our lengthy, rational prayers give way to the prayer of quiet or contemplation. Transition to the next stage often involves the dark night of the spirit.

Third, the way of union with God represents the highest state of integration and spiritual maturity possible in this life. It involves the progressive realization of the "you in me and I in you" union foretold by Jesus in John 14:20. Contemplation, purity of life and love all help to bring about spiritual union. In this third stage believers are still capable of sinning, since we can only reach perfected union in heaven. Each of the three ways, or stages, possesses to some degree features of the other two ways. A person in the illuminative stage, for example, still practices self-denial and spiritual disciplines. The Triple Way journey paradigm remains influential to this day in Roman Catholic and Orthodox circles.

PSEUDO-MACARIUS (FOURTH CENTURY)
This Syrian theologian, valued by many Protestants today, outlined a threefold journey paradigm. First, as a consequence of Adam's rebellion everyone's heart is immersed in evil and in slavery to sin. Only the superior power of divine grace can rescue anyone from such sin. The next stage involves an active spiritual struggle between indwelling sin and God's Spirit. "There are some people in whom grace is operative. . . . Within, however, evil is also present hiddenly, and the two ways of existing, namely according to the principles of light and darkness, vie for dominance in the same heart." Finally, the Spirit casts out the sin that sepa-

rates us from God. The repentant person is united with Christ and "mingled" with the Holy Spirit, thus reversing the Fall and restoring the divine image. Macarius observed that spiritual conflict continues throughout the transformed life. "Satan is never quieted. . . . As long as a person dwells in this world and is living in the flesh, he is subject to warring." The journey envisioned by Macarius progresses "from a heart possessed by evil, to a heart indwelt by sin and grace, and then ultimately to a heart that belongs to God alone."

BERNARD OF CLAIRVAUX (1090-1153)

The French Cistercian abbot, preacher and spiritual director authored many hymns, such as "Jesus, Thou Joy of Loving Hearts," "Jesus, the Very Thought of Thee" and "O Sacred Head Now Wounded." John Calvin appealed widely to Bernard, who has been hailed a reformer four hundred years before the Reformation. In his essay "On the Love of God," Bernard set forth a journey paradigm of developing love in four stages. First, "love of self for self" involves loving oneself (Mt 22:39) as a unique image and likeness of God. If a person fails to love him- or herself appropriately, he or she has little value to impart to others. Bernard designated this foundational stage as one of "immature love."

Second, "love of God for self" involves loving God for the blessings and benefits he brings into our lives. We are attracted to God because he answers prayers, rescues from trouble and satisfies needs. Bernard called this "prudent love."

Third, "love of God for God" involves moving beyond the consolations of God to the God of consolations. Here the soul seeks no reward but God himself. Bernard called this "unselfish love."

The final stage, "love of self for God," involves loving everything, including oneself, in and for God. Bernard called this "perfect love"—a love that offers a foretaste of the love we will enjoy eternally in heaven.

JAN VAN RUYSBROECK (1293-1381)

In *The Spiritual Espousals* and *The Sparkling Stone*, this Flemish spiritual writer mapped out the journey's terrain in four stages. First, Martha exemplifies the "active life," which is oriented to external deeds. Here the journeyer heeds God's commands, follows church disciplines and practices virtue. Second, Martha's sister, Mary, exemplifies the "interior" or "yearning life," which involves intentional and loving pursuit of God in the heart. Third, in the "contemplative life" the journeyer by grace reaches deep union and communion with Christ in a ravishing feast of glory. Finally, the "missional life" occurs when the Christian journeys outward to serve God and others. Since God both works and rests, "anyone [in this stage] who does not possess both rest and activity in one and the same experience has not attained this righteousness."

The Flemish mystic noted, as did earlier authorities, that the stages are cumulative, each assimilating significant features of preceding stages. Persons journeying outward in loving service, for example, continue to practice a vital inner or contemplative life. Van Ruysbroeck designated sojourners in the first three stages, respectively, as "faithful servants" who live an exterior life, "secret friends" who pursue interior life, and "hidden sons" who "see" God via the contemplative life. Progress on the journey involves "the absolute necessity of God's grace and our response to it."

TERESA OF ÁVILA (1515-1582)

In her classic work *The Interior Castle*, the Spanish mystic depicted the journey as a life of deepening prayer in seven stages, imaged by seven rooms of a medieval castle. The journey's end is to abide in the castle's innermost room—the deepest recesses of the soul—where Christ uniquely dwells. Teresa's paradigm draws on the classical triple way and the biblical image of the church as the bride of Christ. Launching the spiritual journey, one enters the castle through the gate of conversion. In rooms one through three of the castle the soul experiences spiritual sweetness by avoiding sin, practicing spiritual disciplines and imitating Jesus. Faith is often weak, prayers are lukewarm, and the soul remains drawn to the world's enticements. God permits the soul to experience dryness in order to wean it from temporal attractions and draw it more deeply to himself. The Christian may remain in this stage for many years.

In rooms four and five the journeyer engages God more intimately through the prayer of quiet recollection. The soul's deepening love and surrender pave the way for profound communion with Christ. Teresa likened the transformation that takes place here to a silkworm that builds its cocoon, dies therein and emerges as a beautiful, white butterfly.

In rooms six and seven the soul is united with its heavenly Spouse. Teresa likened this union to two candles that merge into a single flame and to two beams of sunlight streaming through windows that become a single light. This stage typically involves considerable suffering—taunts by unbelievers, physical afflictions and satanic assaults that increase love for Christ and further purify the soul. Spiritually betrothed to the heavenly Bridegroom, the soul is drawn into the life of the holy Trinity. Here the soul receives a foretaste of heaven and lives out its union with Christ through works of charity.

JOHN OF THE CROSS (1542-1592)

The Spanish saint wrote four major prose works that expound the Christian's journey to God: *The Ascent of Mount Carmel, The Dark Night, Spiritual Canticle* and *Living Flame of Love.* John saw the spiritual journey as a lengthy and often painful process of God purging the old self from worldly attachments and reforming the new self in Christ through a profound union of love.

John portrayed the Christian's spiritual development as occurring in five stages. First, following conversion, the Christian enters the "purgative way," or the "way of beginners." Here the young Christian seeks to please God by mortifying the flesh and practicing verbal prayer and discursive meditation. He or she experiences numerous spiritual comforts, although tending to regard God's blessings as ends in themselves. Paul's portrayal of immature Christians as "infants in Christ" nourished by milk (1 Cor 3:1-2) describes the journeyer in this initial stage. Early in the journey spiritual pride, spiritual gluttony, envy and sloth overwhelm the Christian, as well as a tendency to complacency, sensuality and anger.

Second, the journeyer then enters the purifying dark night of the senses, where he or she is deprived of sensory comforts through a lengthy trial of spiritual dryness. Here the soul is weaned from inferior attachments to worldly gratifications brought into the Christian life from one's preconversion experience. The night of the senses leads the soul to a higher and purer level of maturity and love. Third, the discipline of the sensory dark night leads to a period of consolidation between the two dark nights designated the "illuminative way," or the "way of proficients." Illumined by Christ, the soul recognizes its poverty and the vanity of worldly attractions. By practicing the prayer of quiet, the soul experiences the beginnings of contemplation. The journeyer seeks to imitate Christ and sacrifice for him, although still afflicted with self-seeking, jealousy and unconscious pride in one's achievements.

Fourth, to further purify imperfections God leads the receptive soul into the dark night of the spirit. This second night involves deprivation of sensory and spiritual comforts, purification of false images and memories of God, and purging of lingering vices. This stage also involves a season of questioning and conflict with the world, the flesh and the forces of evil—all of which results in intense suffering. The soul feels abandoned because its former ways of relating to God have been stripped away. The threat at this stage is that the journeyer may despair of spiri-

tual life and abandon faith altogether. The soul progresses, however, by cultivating the prayer of contemplation that leads to
deepened communion with Christ.

Fifth, the dark night of the spirit guides the willing soul into
the "unitive way," or the "way of the perfect." As the journeyer
nears the summit through pure contemplation, the darkness dis-
sipates and the light breaks through, leading to loving union. The
journeyer is raised with Christ and experiences the fire of divine
love in which the three persons of the Trinity are communicated
to the soul. The Christian here experiences an unbroken sense of
God's presence, deep peace amidst trials, and a heart transformed
in faith, hope and charity. In this final stage the soul has entered
into "spiritual marriage." Scripture represents the summit of
union with Christ in texts such as John 17:20-23 and 2 Peter 1:4.
This final stage offers a blissful foretaste of heaven's glory. John
noted that the journey may be halted at any stage; relatively few
Christians in this life attain the unitive way. According to John,
"Everyone knows that not to go forward on this road is to turn
back, and not to gain ground is to lose."

John's fivefold journey paradigm may be represented as follows:

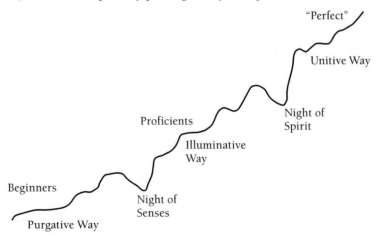

EVELYN UNDERHILL (1875-1941)

The Anglican lay theologian and spiritual writer outlined a five-stage journey paradigm consisting of awakening, purification, illumination, the dark night and union with God. Awakening involves the first yearning of the soul for God accompanied by a burst of joy. Purification signals the painful and humbling stripping of inferior attachments that distance the soul from God. Then follows illumination, involving the Spirit-mediated sense of God's presence in one's life. The journeyer achieves clear and joyful sight of God through contemplation, occasionally accompanied by visions and ecstasies. There follows the dark night of the soul—a season of spiritual crucifixion in which the soul struggles with the painful sense of God's absence. Responding to the dark night redemptively, the Christian surrenders him- or herself to the divine will. Deep relational union with God constitutes the final stage of the mystical way. Underhill observed that the divine Lover is present at every stage of this journey, lovingly wooing the soul to himself.

M. SCOTT PECK (1936-2005)

Informed by the work of James Fowler, psychiatrist M. Scott Peck outlines a four-stage journey paradigm. He designates the first stage as the "Chaotic and Antisocial." Most youth and one in five adults reside here. Adults in this stage ("people of the lie") are self-willed, unprincipled and lacking in integrity. Incapable of loving others, they are "manipulative and self-serving." Because those in this stage are also highly disciplined people, many rise to positions of influence and power. Some advance to the next stage, the "Formal and Institutional," and experience a conversion to Christianity that often is sudden and dramatic. Peck observes that many churchgoers prefer rigid structures and unambiguous formulas to stave off the chaos of stage one. People in this stage tend to be legalistic and fundamentalist—threatened by others who think differently than they do. Stage-two people view God as transcendent rather than immanent and as a disciplinary rather than loving power.

Stage three, the "Skeptic and Individual," reflects a season of serious questioning, as many abandon the formal and legalistic religion of the previous stage. The person here often becomes agnostic about faith. He or she may drop out of church and become consumed with worldly affairs. If the individual seeks truth, a gradual recovery of faith follows. Those who advance to stage four, the "Mystical and Communal," have grown comfortable with God's inscrutability. Exploring the depths of the divine mystery, they relate to God at a deeply intimate level. People in this final stage esteem the world as one large community, or "planetary culture," rather than a host of competing camps.

Peck judges that each journey stage incorporates elements of previous stages. Moreover, a seeker may be attracted to a leader one stage ahead on the journey but intimidated by a person two or more stages ahead. "If they are two steps ahead of us, we usually think they are evil. That's why Socrates and Jesus were killed; they were thought to be evil." Peck attributes progress through the stages to God's gracious initiative and enablement.

JANET HAGBERG AND ROBERT GUELICH

In *The Critical Journey: Stages in the Life of Faith*, Janet O. Hagberg and Robert A. Guelich propose a six-stage paradigm of the spiritual journey. The stages are necessary and progressive, and assume the form of an upward spiral rather than a straight line. First, the pilgrim journey begins with the converted life, involving discovery of God through the new birth. Then follows the learning or discipled life, where apprentices explore and put into practice their new belief system. The third phase is the active or productive life, where the focus is on working diligently for God, often to prove one's worth to oneself or to others. But working *for*

God with less than vital relationship *with* God often leaves the person empty, resentful and exhausted. At the height of "productivity" some experience a crisis due to a developmental event (a midlife transition), an event that intrudes from without (career failure, divorce), a condition that arises from within (burnout, crisis of belief) or a dark night of the soul. Fourth, the crisis prompts an intentional inner journey in which the journeyer seeks God through the practice of renewing spiritual disciplines. Others may experience a crisis or hit a wall while engaging their demons on the inner journey. Fifth, after a significant layer of healing and transformation has occurred, the Spirit faithfully propels the journeyer back into the active world to serve others with renewed vision and purpose. Finally, the Spirit empowers the pilgrim for a life of selfless love, thereby realizing the *summum bonum* (the highest good) of the kingdom of God as commanded by our Lord (Jn 13:34-35).

Notes

Preface

page 12   "Life is a journey": Larry Crabb, *The Safest Place on Earth* (Nashville: Word, 1999), p. 182.

page 13   "When I was a child": The apostle John used descriptors like *children, young people* and *fathers* (1 Jn 2:12-14), likely signifying not age groupings but levels of spiritual maturation.

page 13   The church father Irenaeus: Irenaeus *Against Heresies* 4.11.2, in Ante-Nicene Fathers, ed. Philip Schaff (Grand Rapids: Eerdmans, 1979), 1:474.

page 13   "stage transition dynamics": James Loder, *The Transforming Moment* (San Francisco: Harper & Row, 1981), p. 133.

page 14   eight stages: Erik H. Erikson, *The Life Cycle Completed* (New York: Norton, 1982).

page 14   six sequential stages: Lawrence Kohlberg, *The Psychology of Moral Development* (San Francisco: Harper & Row, 1984).

page 14   six stages of faith development: James Fowler, *Stages of Faith: The Psychology of Human Development and the Quest for Meaning* (San Francisco: Harper & Row, 1981); and *Becoming Adult, Becoming Christian: Adult Development and the Christian Faith* (San Francisco: Jossey-Bass, 2000).

page 15   threefold pattern: Walter Brueggemann, *Praying the Psalms* (Winona, Minn.: Saint Mary's, 1982).

page 15   "three foundational moments": Richard Byrne, "Journey (Growth and Development in Spiritual Life)," in *The New Dictionary of Catholic Spirituality*, ed. Michael Downey (Collegeville, Minn.: Liturgical Press, 1993), p. 568.

Chapter 1: Initial Orientation

page 19   theatrical shows: Augustine *Confessions* 2.2.2, in *Writings of St. Augustine*, The Fathers of the Church, trans. John A. Mourant and William J. Collinge (Washington, D.C.: Catholic University of America Press, 1953), 5:34.

page 19   recognized to be the triune God: Augustine *Confessions* 3.1.1, in *Writings of St. Augustine*, 5:49.

page 20   "light of peace flooding": Augustine *Confessions* 8.12.29, in *Writings of St. Augustine*, 5:224-25.

page 20   like so many atheists: C. S. Lewis, *Surprised by Joy* (New York: Book of the Month Club, 1992), p. 115.

page 20   "admitted that God was God": Lewis, *Surprised*, pp. 228-29.

page 20   the spiritual journey begins: For the grace of God that brings salvation, see Eph 2:7-8 and Tit 2:11.

page 22   though we are complete in Christ: For believers brought to "fullness" in Christ, see Col 2:10.

page 22   old self . . . new self: For believers in Christ putting off the "old self" and putting on the "new self," see Eph 4:22-24 and Col 3:9-10.

page 23   "How great is the fervor": Thomas à Kempis *The Imitation of Christ* 1.18, ed. Donald E. Demaray (Grand Rapids: Baker, 1982), p. 40.

page 23   experience as new Christians: John of the Cross *Dark Night of the Soul* 1.1 (New York: Doubleday/Image, 1990), p. 38.

page 23   "The old man, alas": Thomas à Kempis *The Imitation of Christ* 3.34 (Peabody, Mass.: Hendrickson, 2004), p. 96.

page 24   Peter walked with Jesus: For Peter's spiritual immaturity, see Mt 14:28-31; 16:22-23; 26:40, 43, 45, 51, 69-74.

page 25   John Bishop: "Families Unite in Grief Over Slayings," *Denver Post*, April 8, 2001, p. 1B.

page 26   offensive manifestations of the old nature: For warnings against sexual immorality, see Rom 13:13; 1 Cor 5:1; 6:18;

2 Cor 12:21; Gal 5:19; Eph 5:3; 1 Thess 4:3; Heb 13:4.

page 26   no longer enslave us as God's children: For believers delivered from bondage to sin, see Rom 6:6-7, 14, 16-18.

pages 26-27   "human being is seduced": Dennis Prager, *Happiness Is a Serious Problem* (New York: HarperCollins/Regan, 1998), p. 43.

page 27   "attachment to created things": Thomas à Kempis *Imitation of Christ* 2.1, pp. 36-37.

page 27   seek fulfillment apart from . . . God: For the ultimate emptiness of worldly possessions and pleasures, see Eccles 2:1-11.

page 28   "New Christians": François Fénelon, *Meditations and Devotions*, cited in Bernard Bangley, *Nearer to the Heart of God* (Brewster, Mass.: Paraclete, 2005), p. 10.

page 29   American culture's emphasis on excessive working: A recent Harvard study revealed that the average American works 46.2 weeks a year, the average Frenchman 40.5 weeks and the average Swede 35.4 weeks. Craig Wilson, "Who Needs the Baggage? Here's to Staying Put," *USA Today*, August 23, 2006, p. 1D.

page 30   Christians who left the church: See William D. Hendricks, *Exit Interviews: Revealing Stories of Why People Are Leaving the Church* (Chicago: Moody Press, 1993), p. 261.

page 30   "the fundamental verb, to Be": Evelyn Underhill, *Essential Writings* (Maryknoll, N.Y.: Orbis, 2003), p. 31.

page 30   "slowing down": Underhill, *Essential Writings*, p. 52.

page 30   lacking mature knowledge: For immature knowledge of the Christian way, see Heb 6:1-2.

page 31   "Many of these beginners": Cited in *Saint John of the Cross for Every Day* (New York: Paulist, 2007), p. 28.

page 33   seven capital sins: John of the Cross *Dark Night of the Soul*, bk. 1, chaps. 2-7, in *Collected Works*, trans. Kieran Kavanaugh and Otilio Rodriguez (Washington, D.C.: ICS, 1991), pp. 362-75.

page 33   "children who kick and cry": John of the Cross *Ascent of Mount Carmel*, in *Collected Works*, pp. 115-16.

page 33   "feebleness of their state": John of the Cross *Dark Night* 1.1.1, in *Collected Works*, p. 361.

page 33   "similar their deeds are": John of the Cross *Dark Night* 1.1.3, in *Collected Works*, p. 362.

page 34   a plan for spiritual growth: George Barna, *Growing True Disciples* (Colorado Springs: WaterBrook, 2001), p. 49.

page 34   "what faith maturity looks like": "Christians Say They Do Best at Relationships, Worst in Bible Knowledge," June 14, 2005 <www.barna.org>.

page 34   "Free from the law, O happy condition": Philip P. Bliss, "Free from the Law" (1871).

page 35   the rule of love: For the rule of love enjoined by Jesus and his apostles see Mt 5:43-44; Rom 13:9-10; 1 Pet 1:22; 1 Jn 4:11-12.

page 36   Satan's seductions: John Calvin *Institutes of the Christian Religion* 1.14.13, in Library of Christian Classics, trans. Henry Beveridge (Philadelphia: Westminster Press, 1960), 1:173.

page 36   younger adults are withdrawing: "Most Twentysomethings Put Christianity on the Shelf Following Spiritually Active Teen Years," September 11, 2006 <www.barna .org>.

page 37   "become a little Christ": C. S. Lewis, *Mere Christianity* (New York: Macmillan, 1952), p. 153.

page 37   pass through the desert: John Chrysostom *Homilies on Ephesians* 23, in *Nicene and Post Nicene Fathers* 1.13, ed. Philip Schaff (Grand Rapids: Eerdmans, 1979), pp. 165-66.

Chapter 2: Painful Disorientation: Seasons of Distress

page 41   "Prosperity knits a person": C. S. Lewis, *The Screwtape Letters* (London: Geoffrey Bles, 1961), p. 124.

page 41   "To live is to suffer": Cited by Dennis Prager, *Happiness is a Serious Problem* (New York: HarperCollins/Regan, 1998), p. 54.

page 41   Peter alerted scattered saints: For trials, persecutions and sufferings, see 1 Peter 1:6; 5:9-10.

page 41   "absolute security and peace": Thomas à Kempis *The Imitation of Christ*, in *Nearer to the Heart of God*, ed. Bernard Bangley (Brewster, Mass.: Paraclete, 2005), p. 175.

page 41   "So long as we live": Thomas à Kempis *The Imitation of Christ* 1.13, trans. Donald Demaray (Grand Rapids: Baker, 1982), p. 28.

page 42   fourth-century monk: Pseudo-Macarius, *Homily* 15.12, in

Pseudo-Macarius: The Fifty Spiritual Homilies and the Great Letter, trans. and ed. George A. Maloney, Classics of Western Spirituality (New York: Paulist, 1992), p. 112.

page 42 　"trouble": New International Dictionary of New Testament Theology, ed. Colin Brown (Grand Rapids: Zondervan, 1981), 2:807.

page 43 　emotionally distressed and weakened: Walter Brueggemann, Praying the Psalms (Winona, Minn.: Saint Mary's Press, 1982), pp. 18, 20.

page 46 　"found hell rather than heaven": William L. Lane, The Gospel of Mark, New International Commentary on the New Testament (London: Marshall, Morgan & Scott, 1974), p. 516.

page 47 　Paul . . . on his mission journeys: Paul cites his many trials in 2 Cor 1:6-10; 4:8-12; 6:4-5, 9-10; 11:23-27; Eph 3:13.

page 47 　first-century believers: For the travail first-century Christians suffered see Heb 4:15; 10:33; 12:7; Jas 1:2; 1 Pet 4:12.

pages 47-48 　martyred for Christ: See the website of The Voice of the Martyrs: <www.persecution.org>.

page 48 　reflecting on his own times: Pseudo-Macarius The Fifty Spiritual Homilies 9.7, p. 85.

page 48 　"pulling the flesh from my bones": Mark Galli and Ted Olsen, eds., 131 Christians Everyone Should Know (Nashville: Broadman & Holman, 2000), p. 116.

page 48 　"my spirit so filled with darkness": See Thomas J. Heffernan, "Biographies, Spiritual," in The New Westminster Dictionary of Christian Spirituality, ed. Philip Sheldrake (Louisville, Ky.: Westminster John Knox, 2005), p. 150.

page 49 　leading Christians who suffered: Many other Christians who suffered severe trials could be mentioned, such as Julian of Norwich (c. 1342-1416), John Donne (1572-1631), John Newton (1725-1807), Watchman Nee (1903-1972) and Richard Wurmbrand (1909-2001). Their heroic lives are worth reading.

page 50 　"shipshape, clear, and comfortable": Friedrich von Hügel, Letters to a Niece (New York: J. M. Dent, 1928), p. xvi.

page 51 　"God instructs the heart": Jean Pierre de Caussade, The

Sacrament of the Present Moment (New York: HarperSan-
Francisco, 1989), p. 51.

page 52   "Suffering is the greatest teacher": Hügel, Letters, p. xv.

page 52   "Plant yourself": Ibid., p. xliii.

page 53   as fire purifies gold: For biblical images describing refin-
               ing of character, see Jer 13:24; Joel 3:13; Jn 15:2; 1 Pet 1:7.

page 53   "the Holy Spirit uses tribulation": William Tyndale, Pref-
               ace to Obedience, cited in Bangley, Nearer to the Heart of
               God, pp. 263-64.

pages 53-54   "The more we are afflicted": John Calvin Institutes of the
               Christian Religion 3.8.1, Library of Christian Classics, trans.
               Henry Beveridge (Philadelphia: Westminster Press, 1960),
               1:702.

page 55   "severe mercy": See C. S. Lewis's letter to Sheldon
               Vanauken, in Vanauken, A Severe Mercy (San Francisco:
               Harper & Row, 1977), pp. 209-10.

page 55   "The world says": François Fénelon, "Set Me Free," in
               Meditations on the Heart of God (Brewster, Mass.: Para-
               clete, 1997), p. 167.

page 55   "The holiest of all": John Wycliffe, in Bangley, Nearer to
               the Heart of God, pp. 11-12.

page 56   Simeon the Stylite: Cited in Ariel Glucklich, Sacred Pain
               (New York: Oxford University Press, 2001), p. 24.

page 56   Bernard of Clairvaux: Cited by P. Camporesi, The Incor-
               ruptible Flesh (Cambridge: Cambridge University Press,
               1988), p. 110.

page 56   Henry Suso: See John T. McNeill and Helen M. Gamer,
               eds., Medieval Handbook of Penance (New York: Columbia
               University Press, 1938), p. 354.

page 57   "extremely unmortified": Caussade, Sacrament, p. xvii.

page 57   "suffering avoidance": Richard J. Foster, "Growing
               Edges," Renovaré 16, no. 1 (February 2006): 1.

page 58   common apostolic theme: For Christians suffering with
               Christ see Rom 8:17; 2 Cor 1:5; Phil 3:10.

page 58   "if this was God's way on earth": Francis of Assisi, cited
               in Prayers and Meditations of Thérèse of Lisieux (Ann Ar-
               bor, Mich.: Servant, 1992), p. 91.

page 59   William Cowper: "Light Shining Out of Darkness," Fire
               and Ice: Puritan and Reformed Writings <www.puritan
               sermons.com/poetry/cowper8.htm>.

Chapter 3: Painful Disorientation: Understanding Why We Suffer

page 61   "the great variety of punishments": Augustine *The City of God* 22.22, in *Writings of St. Augustine*, The Fathers of the Church, trans. John A. Mourant and William J. Collinge (Washington, D.C.: Catholic University of America Press, 1966), 8:474.

page 62   Unconfessed sin: Other Scriptures that link sin with ineffectiveness in prayer include Prov 1:28; Is 1:15.

page 62   "Tiny sins will not": Francis of Sales, *An Introduction to the Devout Life*, cited in Bernard Bangley, *Nearer to the Heart of God* (Brewster, Mass.: Paraclete, 2005), p. 16.

page 63   "If you break God's law": Christopher Love, *The Dejected Soul's Cure*, cited in Peter Lewis, *The Genius of Puritanism* (Haywards Heath, U.K.: Carey, 1975), p. 79.

page 63   "Concealed guilt": Christopher Love, *Grace: The Truth and Growth*, cited in Lewis, *Genius of Puritanism*, p. 80.

page 63   Moses warned the Israelites: See Deut 28:15-68.

page 64   Greek words for world: The two words for world are *aion* ("age," more than 100 times) and *kosmos* ("world order, system," 185 times).

page 64   principles hostile to God: For the world order hostile to God and his people see Jn 17:14; Jas 4:4; 1 Jn 3:13.

page 64   because we are citizens of another world: John Calvin *Institutes of the Christian Religion* 3.8.7, in Library of Christian Classics, trans. Henry Beveridge (Philadelphia: Westminster Press, 1960), 1:707-8.

page 66   "It is Satan's practice": Richard Sibbes, *The Works of Richard Sibbes* (Edinburgh: Banner of Truth, 1973), 1:142.

page 67   biblical examples of Satan's solicitations: For indications of Satan's enticements to sin see 1 Chron 21:1; Jn 13:2; Acts 5:3.

page 68   "cannot keep you from having grace": Love, *Dejected Soul's Cure,* cited in Lewis, *Genius of Puritanism*, p. 92.

page 70   Dissatisfaction with life: A June 20, 2008, edition of the ABC television program *Nightline* reported the results of detailed studies by social scientists from many countries on the subject of happiness and unhappiness. The research consistently showed that men and women in their forties are the least happy, with age 44 as the unhappiest in the human life cycle.

page 70   midlife crisis: Different experts apply different age
               ranges: for example, thirty-five to forty (Jung), thirty-
               five to forty-five (Levinson and Sheehy), or thirty-five to
               fifty-five (Conway).

page 71   "simply tired of having a tired body": Jim Conway, *Men in
               Mid Life Crisis* (Elgin, Ill.: Cook, 1978), p. 57.

page 71   Ambitious goals . . . seem unachievable: Janice Brewi and
               Anne Brennan, *Mid-Life: Psychological and Spiritual Per-
               spectives* (New York: Crossroad, 1982), p. 39.

page 72   "not knowing who we are at all": Brewi and Brennan,
               Mid-Life, p. 53.

page 72   "cannot live the afternoon of life": Nancy Meyer, *The
               Male Mid-Life Crisis* (Garden City, N.Y.: Doubleday, 1978),
               p. 248.

page 72   Puritan pastors and theologians: Lewis, *Genius of Puri-
               tanism*, p. 71.

page 74   God had planned and executed: For Jeremiah's claim
               that Israel's calamities were sent by God see Lam 2:17;
               3:38.

page 74   "God's way of fertilizing": Martin Luther, *Sermons on the
               Gospel of St. John: Chapter 14-16*, in *Luther's Works*, ed.
               Jaroslav Pelikan (St. Louis: Concordia, 1955-86), 24:195.

page 74   God has "sometimes sent us sickness": Jan van Ruys-
               broeck, *The Spiritual Espousals and Other Works*, ed.
               James A. Wiseman, Classics of Western Spirituality (New
               York: Paulist Press, 1985), p. 80.

page 74   "do not consider yourself forsaken": Thomas à Kempis
               Imitation of Christ 3.30.5 (Peabody, Mass.: Hendrickson,
               2004), p. 91.

page 74   "God is a clever designer of crosses": François Fénelon,
               Meditations and Devotions, cited in Bangley, *Nearer to the
               Heart of God*, p. 183.

page 76   Peter's first letter: For Peter's teachings on suffering see
               1 Pet 1:6; 2:19-21; 3:17; 4:12-19; 5:9.

page 76   "When God wants to build": Martin Luther, cited in
               Ewald M. Plass, *What Luther Says* (St. Louis: Concordia,
               1959), p. 21.

page 77   painful education of his children: Calvin *Institutes* 3.8.6,
               1:706; see also 3.8.11, 1:711.

Chapter 4: Painful Disorientation: Dark Night of the Soul

page 80   "suffering has to be punishment": Martin E. Marty, *A Cry of Absence: Reflections on the Winter of the Heart* (San Francisco: Harper & Row, 1983), p. 139.

page 80   "Why, O God": Ibid., p. 147.

page 80   desolation resulting from God's hiddenness: On this, see Job 29:3 and Ps 44:19. Other figurative meanings of darkness include disaster (Mk 13:24), the sinful state (Rom 13:12; 1 Thess 5:5) and an evil power (Col 1:13; Eph 5:8).

page 81   Job's magnificent confession: "I know that my redeemer lives, / and that in the end he will stand on the earth. / And after my skin has been destroyed, / yet in my flesh I will see God" (Job 19:25-26).

page 85   "you broke her body": C. S. Lewis, *A Grief Observed* (New York: Bantam, 1976), p. 49.

page 85   "Cosmic Sadist": Ibid., pp. 35, 43-45, 49.

page 85   "unreasonableness, vanity . . .": Ibid., p. 37.

page 85   "Why is He so present": Ibid., p. 5.

page 85   "the painful silence": See James Emery White, *Embracing the Mysterious God* (Downers Grove, Ill.: InterVarsity Press, 2003), pp. 65-67.

page 85   "profound interior suffering": See *Mother Teresa: Come Be My Light*, ed. Brian Kolodiejchuk (New York: Doubleday, 2007), pp. 21-22.

page 85   "I have come to love the darkness": "Mother Teresa Tormented by Crisis of Faith," *The Denver Post*, August 26, 2007, p. 2A.

page 86   "After we have been": Oswald Chambers, *My Utmost for His Highest* (Uhrichsville, Ohio: Barbour, n.d.), April 4.

page 86   "I fell into a depression": Lewis B. Smedes, *My God and I: A Spiritual Memoir* (Grand Rapids: Eerdmans, 2003), p. 131.

page 86   "God came back to me": Ibid., p. 132.

page 87   "Here I was . . . flat on the ground": Henri J. M. Nouwen, *The Inner Voice of Love: A Journey Through Anguish to Freedom* (New York: Doubleday/Image, 1998), p. xiii.

page 87   must be stripped of earthly attachments: See John of the Cross *The Dark Night* 1.1.2, in *The Collected Works of Saint John of the Cross*, trans. Kieran Kavanaugh and Otilio

Rodriguez (Washington, D.C.: ICS, 1991), p. 361.

page 88   "passive night of the senses": Gerald May, *The Dark Night of the Soul* (New York: HarperSanFrancisco, 2005), p. 86.

page 88   peaceful period: John of the Cross *Dark Night* 2.1.1, in *Collected Works*, p. 395.

page 89   "become so attached to feelings": May, *Dark Night of the Soul*, p. 93.

page 89   "purification of the will through charity": John of the Cross *Ascent of Mount Carmel* 3.16.1, in *Collected Works*, pp. 291-92.

page 90   "What the sorrowing soul": John of the Cross *Dark Night* 2.6.2, in *Collected Works*, p. 404.

page 90   many experience the sensory night: John of the Cross *Dark Night* 1.8.1, in *Collected Works*, p. 375.

page 90   God sometimes afflicts: Cited in Ewald M. Plass, ed., *What Luther Says* (St. Louis: Concordia, 1959), p. 241.

pages 90-91 Swiss reformer John Calvin: John Calvin, *Institutes of the Christian Religion* 3.20.3, in Library of Christian Classics, trans. Henry Beveridge (Philadelphia: Westminster Press, 1960), 2:853.

page 91   strip away our self-sufficiency: G. A. Hemming, "The Puritans' Dealings with Troubled Souls," in Martyn Lloyd-Jones, *Puritan Papers: Volume One 1956-1959* (Phillipsburg, N.J.: P & R, 2000), p. 35.

page 91   "When a child of God is truly walking": Ibid., p. 37.

page 91   "One who truly fears God": Thomas Goodwin, *A Child of Light Walking in Darkness* (London: A. Dawlman & L. Fawne, 1638), pp. 5-6.

page 91   A. W. Tozer described the dark night: A. W. Tozer, *The Divine Conquest* (New York: Revell, 1959), p. 126.

page 91   "If we cooperate with God": Ibid., p. 125.

pages 91-92 "The value of the stripping experience": Ibid., p. 126.

page 92   Why does God so treat his saints: William Bridge, *A Lifting Up for the Downcast* (London: Banner of Truth Trust, 1979), p. 176.

page 92   the Valley of the Shadow of Death: John Bunyan, *The Pilgrim's Progress*, ed. Hal M. Helms, in *Christian Classics/Living Library* (Brewster, Mass.: Paraclete, 1982), p. 113.

page 92   "utterly without order": Ibid., p. 110.

page 93   As for why God absents himself: François Fénelon, *The*

Royal Way of the Cross (Brewster, Mass.: Paraclete, 1982), p. 23.

page 93   Peter's cowardly denial of Christ: David Crowner and Gerald Christianson, eds., *The Spirituality of the German Awakening*, Classics of Western Spirituality (New York: Paulist Press, 2003), p. 95.

page 93   Gerald May helpfully defined the dark night: May, *Dark Night of the Soul*, pp. 4-5.

page 93   "a totally loving, healing, and liberating process": Ibid., p. 68.

page 94   "God has moved away": See *Upper Room Dictionary of Christian Spiritual Formation*, ed. Keith Beasley-Topliffe (Nashville: Upper Room, 2003), p. 89.

pages 94-95   "vital to a man's development": Daniel Levinson, *The Seasons of a Man's Life* (New York: Ballantine, 1978), p. 30.

page 95   "The point of our crises and calamities": Kathleen Norris, *The Cloister Walk* (New York: Riverhead, 1996), p. 213.

page 95   a "transforming moment": James E. Loder, *The Transforming Moment* (San Francisco: Harper & Row, 1981).

page 96   "crucial marker events": Levinson, *Seasons of a Man's Life*, p. 61; see also pp. 54-56.

pages 96-97   Gerald May comments: May, *Dark Night of the* Soul, p. 180.

page 97   "too many noes": Nouwen, *Inner Voice of Love*, p. 28.

page 98   dark night of the soul and clinical depression: Depression is indicated in Scriptures such as Ps 42:5-6, 11; Prov 18:14.

page 98   "depression is a psychological sickness": Thomas Moore, *Dark Nights of the Soul* (New York: Gotham, 2004), p. xiv.

page 98   sense the reality of God's wisdom: Gerald M. May, *Care of Mind/Care of Spirit* (New York: HarperSanFrancisco, 1992), p. 110.

pages 98-99   other potential causes of darkness: John of the Cross *Dark Night* 1.9, in *Collected Works*, pp. 377-80.

page 99   "dark night of the soul takes you to Hell": Moore, *Dark Nights*, p. 114; see also pp. 57, 67.

page 100   "The dark fire of God": John of the Cross, *Living Flame of*

Love, in David Hazard, *You Set My Spirit Free* (Minneapolis: Bethany House, 1994), p. 57.

page 100   "In the dark night": Moore, *Dark Nights*, p. 5.

page 100   "Delightful feelings": John of the Cross *Letter 13*, in *Collected Works*, p. 747.

page 101   the cup of desolation: Hemming, "The Puritans' Dealings," p. 43.

page 101   Pope John Paul II encouraged: Cited in "Defining the Language of Life, Death," *USA Today*, October 5, 2005, p. 6D.

Chapter 5: Painful Disorientation: Redemptive Responses

page 104   *lectio divina:* The discipline of *lectio divina*, practiced by Christians since the fourth century, includes careful reading of a biblical text *(lectio)*, meditating on what is read *(meditatio)*, praying portions of the Scripture back to God *(oratio)*, resting in God *(contemplatio)*, and living out the Word read *(incarnatio)*. For an excellent explanation of *lectio*, see Eugene H. Peterson, *Eat This Book* (Grand Rapids: Eerdmans, 2006), pp. 90-117.

page 105   "what he ordains for us": Jean Pierre de Caussade, *The Sacrament of the Present Moment* (New York: HarperSanFrancisco: 1982), p. 42.

page 106   a higher judge than God: Wayne Martindale and Jerry Root, eds., *The Quotable Lewis* (Wheaton, Ill.: Tyndale House, 1989), p. 221.

page 106   "Our sense of unworthiness": Thelma Hall, *Too Deep for Words* (New York: Paulist, 1988), p. 54.

page 107   Barna research: "The Concept of Holiness Baffles Most Americans," February 20, 2006 <www.barna.org>.

page 107   "The soul is cast down too much": Richard Sibbes, *The Works of Richard Sibbes* (Edinburgh: Banner of Truth, 1982), 7:52.

page 109   "Gently turn to Him": Friedrich von Hügel, *Letters to a Niece* (London: J. M. Dent, 1958), p. 93.

page 110   "God cannot bless us": Martindale and Root, *Quotable Lewis*, p. 172.

page 110   C. S. Lewis made this point: C. S. Lewis, *Mere Christianity* 4.8, cited in Martindale and Root, *Quotable Lewis*, p. 571.

page 112   "a wintry sort of spirituality": Martin E. Marty, *A Cry of Absence* (San Francisco: Harper & Row, 1983), p. 153.

page 113   know the Shepherd's voice: For Jesus' teaching that his sheep recognize the voice of the Shepherd see Jn 10:3-5, 27.

page 113   The hard truth: François Fénelon, *Meditations on the Heart of God* (Brewster, Mass.: Paraclete, 1997), p. 69.

page 114   "no life without death": Hügel, *Letters*, p. xliii.

page 114   "no remedy for this darkness": Caussade, *Sacrament of the Present Moment*, p. 17.

page 114   "Do not go abroad": Augustine "On True Religion" 72, in *Augustine: Earlier Writings*, ed. John S. Burleigh, Library of Christian Classics (Philadelphia: Westminster Press, 1953), 6:262.

page 114   Protestants tend to overlook: Elizabeth O'Connor, for example, acknowledged that "in Protestantism it is very difficult to find any help in drawing closer to the real self" (*Journey Inward, Journey Outward* [New York: Harper & Row, 1968], p. 29).

page 115   "A certain slowing down": Evelyn Underhill, *Essential Writings*, ed. Emilie Griffin (Maryknoll, N.Y.: Orbis, 2003), p. 52.

page 115   "Who is likely to be": Dennis Prager, *Happiness Is a Serious Problem* (New York: Harper Collins/Regan, 1998), pp. 109-10.

pages 115-16   "cannot organize or manipulate God": Henri J. M. Nouwen, *Reaching Out* (New York: Doubleday, 1975), p. 126.

page 117   "Prayer is really an attitude": Ole Hallesby, *Prayer* (Minneapolis: Augsburg, 1931), pp. 146-47.

page 118   "involuntary askesis": Eugene H. Peterson, *Under the Unpredictable Plant* (Grand Rapids: Eerdmans, 1992), p. 89.

page 118   redemption from the plague of sin: For God's deliverance from various forms of oppression and distress see Ex 18:10; Ps 18:47-48; 103:2-4; 124.

page 120   recent study: Janet Kornblum, "Study: 25% of Americans Have No One to Confide In," *USA Today*, June 23-25, 2006, p. 1A.

page 121   "sets himself up as his own teacher": Bernard of Clairvaux "Letter XXIV," in *Some Letters of Saint Bernard, Abbot of Clairvaux* (London: John Hodges, 1904), p. 102.

page 123	Hügel urged distressed souls: Hügel, *Letters*, p. xlv.
page 123	persevere in their hardships: For biblical commands to be courageous see Josh 1:7; 10:25; Mt 14:27; Acts 23:11; 1 Cor 16:13.
page 123	persevere with unwavering faith: Jeremiah Burroughs, cited in Peter Lewis, *The Genius of Puritanism* (Haywards Heath, U.K.: Carey, 1975), p. 134.
page 124	verses from a saint who suffered: William Cowper, "The Saints Should Never Be Dismayed," verses 1 and 6; <www.cyberhymnal.org/htm/s/a/saintssn.htm>.

Chapter 6: Joyful Reorientation

page 128	illumines the soul's shadows: Although Scriptures such as Isaiah 58:8, 10; 60:1 historically describe Israel's restoration from captivity, they anticipate the spiritual enlightening and well-being God bestows upon his trusting people.
page 128	a log set on fire: John of the Cross *The Living Flame of Love*, Prologue 3, in *The Collected Works of St. John of the Cross*, trans. Kieran Kavanaugh and Otilio Rodriguez (Washington, D.C.: ICS, 1991), p. 639.
page 129	One Puritan wrote: Nathaniel Whiting, cited in Peter Lewis, *The Genius of Puritanism* (Haywards Heath, U.K.: Carey, 1975), p. 85.
page 129	God's face reappeared: C. S. Lewis, *A Grief Observed* (New York: Bantam, 1976), pp. 51-52.
pages 129-30	Peterson notes: Eugene H. Peterson, *Christ Plays in Ten Thousand Places* (Grand Rapids: Eerdmans, 2005), p. 232.
page 130	Christ's powerful resurrection life: For evidence that reoriented believers are caught up in Christ's resurrection life see Rom 8:11; Eph 1:18-21.
page 130	emerges as a beautiful butterfly: Teresa of Ávila, *Interior Castle*, in *The Collected Works of St. Teresa of Avila*, trans. Kieran Kavanaugh and Otilio Rodriguez (Washington, D.C.: ICS, 1980), 2:341-44.
page 130	Barna Group: "The Concept of Holiness Baffles Most Americans," February 20, 2006 <www.barna.org>.
page 131	After her healing Julian wrote: Julian of Norwich, *Revela-*

tions of Divine Love, trans. Elizabeth Spearing (London: Penguin, 1998), p. 90.

page 131   restoration inspired her to write: Julian of Norwich, Showings, trans. Edmund Colledge and James Walsh, Classics of Western Spirituality (New York: Paulist, 1978), p. 225.

page 131   union with Christ: For the "in Christ" language of the New Testament see Jn 14:20; Rom 8:10; Col 1:27.

page 132   "a total transformation": John of the Cross Spiritual Canticle 22.3, in Collected Works, p. 560.

page 133   hymn by Charles Wesley: Charles Wesley, in John and Charles Wesley, ed. Frank Whaling, Classics of Western Spirituality (New York: Paulist, 1981), p. 27.

page 134   divinization . . . synonym for sanctification: The Theologia Germanica of Martin Luther, trans. Bengt Hoffman, Classics of Western Spirituality (New York: Paulist, 1980), pp. 104, 106-7, 110-11, 120, 122, 127-28.

page 134   "The deepest desire of our hearts": Brennan Manning, Abba's Child: The Cry of the Heart for Intimate Belonging (Colorado Springs: NavPress, 1994), pp. 38-39.

page 135   peace Jesus gave: For Jesus' bestowal of peace upon his followers see Jn 14:27; 20:19, 21, 26.

page 135   "you have a right to peace": Cited in Lewis, Genius of Puritanism, p. 108.

page 136   No longer ashamed of Christ: For evidence of Peter's transformation in the order here stated see 1 Pet 3:3-4; 2 Pet 1:5-6; 1 Pet 5:10; 2 Pet 1:16-18; 1 Pet 3:14; 1 Pet 4:16.

pages 138-39   Thérèse of Lisieux . . . "little Way": Doris R. Leckey, Seven Essentials for the Spiritual Journey (New York: Crossroad, 1999), p. 103.

page 139   the genre of imaginative fiction: See also William Bouwsma, "Christian Adulthood," in Adulthood, ed. Erik H. Erikson (New York: Norton, 1978), pp. 91-92, cited in Les L. Steele, On the Way (Grand Rapids: Baker, 1990), pp. 31-32.

page 139   "a paradoxical ideal of maturity": Evelyn Eaton and James D. Whitehead, Christian Life Patterns (Garden City, N.Y.: Doubleday, 1979), p. 149.

page 140   "the journey inward . . . the journey outward": Robert E. Webber, God Still Speaks (Nashville: Thomas Nelson, 1980), p. 171.

page 142	"contemplatives of all traditions agree": Gerald G. May, *The Dark Night of the Soul* (New York: HarperSanFrancisco, 2004), p. 182.
page 142	four elements of *agapē* love: Joseph M. Stowell, *Shepherding the Church* (Chicago: Moody, 1997), pp. 181-82.
page 143	"I love you alone": Augustine *Soliloquies* 1.1.5, in *Writings of Saint Augustine*, ed. Ludwig Schopp, Fathers of the Church (New York: CIMA, 1948), 1:348.
page 143	"O Lord, I love you": Augustine *Sermon* 159.8, cited in *Augustine Day by Day*, ed. John Rotelle (New York: Catholic Book, 1986), p. 14.
page 143	"soaked and engulfed in love": Thérèse of Lisieux, *Prayers and Meditations*, ed. Cindy Cavnar (Ann Arbor, Mich.: Servant, 1992), p. 32.
page 143	"All is fleeting": Ibid., p. 46.
page 145	"examined in love": John of the Cross *The Sayings of Light and Love* 60, in *Collected Works*, p. 90.
page 146	Augustine . . . savoring eternity: Augustine *On the Gospel of John* 40.10, in *Nicene and Post-Nicene Fathers,* ed. Philip Schaff (Peabody, Mass.: Hendrickson, 1994), 7:228-29.
page 147	failure to experience the joy of reorientation: John of the Cross *Living Flame of Love* 2.27, in *Collected Works*, p. 667.
page 148	"there are always two notes": Friedrich von Hügel, *Letters of Friedrich von Hügel to a Niece* (New York: J. M. Dent, 1928), p. xix.

Chapter 7: Conclusion

page 151	The word *mature:* Greek, *teleios.* For Scriptures indicating that spiritual maturity involves wholeness or completeness see 1 Kings 8:61; Jas 1:4.
page 151	Our course on the journey: Augustine *Christian Instruction* 1.34, in *Writings of Saint Augustine*, vol. 2, Fathers of the Church (Washington, D.C.: Catholic University of America Press, 1947), p. 55.
page 152	prayer penned by a Puritan divine: Arthur Bennett, ed., *The Valley of Vision: A Collection of Puritan Prayers and Devotions* (Edinburgh: Banner of Truth, 1975), p. 1.
page 153	Believers experience "labors and sorrows": Thomas à Kempis *The Imitation of Christ* 3.35 (Peabody, Mass.: Hendrickson, 2004), p. 97.

page 153   "I owe everything to the furnace": Charles H. Spurgeon,
                "And We Are," in *The Metropolitan Tabernacle Pulpit* (Pas-
                adena, Tex.: Pilgrim, 1974), 2:683.

page 153   "prosperity and pleasure": Abraham Kuyper, *Near Unto
                God* (Grand Rapids: CRC, 1997), p. 113.

pages 154-55   Mother Teresa: See Carol Zaleski, "The Dark Night of
                Mother Teresa," *First Things* 133, no. 1 (May 2003): 25.

page 155   "orientation, disorientation, and reorientation": Walter
                Brueggemann, *Praying the Psalms*, 2nd ed. (Eugene, Ore.:
                Wipf & Stock, 2007), p. 3.

page 156   Teresa of Ávila's prudent counsel: Cited in Gerald May,
                The Dark Night of the Soul (New York: HarperSanFran-
                cisco, 2004), p. 187.

pages 156-57   "We never arrive": Adrian van Kaam, *The Tender Farewell
                of Jesus* (Hyde Park, N.Y.: New City, 1996), p. 18.

Appendix

pages 160-61   "Triple Way" paradigm: See Benedict Groeschel, *Spiri-
                tual Passages: The Psychology of Spiritual Development*
                (New York: Crossroad, 1993). Some Protestants affirm
                the value of this paradigm, such as M. Robert Mulhol-
                land Jr., *Invitation to a Journey: A Road Map for Spiritual
                Formation* (Downers Grove, Ill.: InterVarsity Press, 1993),
                chap. 8.

page 161   consequence of Adam's rebellion: Pseudo-Macarius *Hom-
                ily* 15.35-36, in *Pseudo-Macarius: The Fifty Spiritual Hom-
                ilies and the Great Letter*, trans. and ed. George A. Malo-
                ney, Classics of Western Spirituality (New York: Paulist,
                1992), p. 121.

page 161   active spiritual struggle: Pseudo-Macarius *Homily* 17.4,
                in *Fifty Spiritual Homilies*, p. 137.

page 162   restoring the divine image: Pseudo-Macarius *Homily*
                32.6, in *Fifty Spiritual Homilies*, p. 199.

page 162   "Satan is never quieted": Pseudo-Macarius *Homily* 26.14,
                in *Fifty Spiritual Homilies*, p. 169.

page 162   "a heart that belongs to God alone": Kallistos Ware, pref-
                ace to *Fifty Spiritual Homilies*, p. xiii.

page 163   "missional life": Jan van Ruysbroeck, *The Spiritual Espous-
                als and Other Works*, ed. James A. Wiseman, Classics of
                Western Spirituality (New York: Paulist, 1985), p. 135.

page 163   progress on the journey: Van Ruysbroeck, *Spiritual Espousals*, p. 120.

page 166   relatively few . . . attain the unitive way: For a helpful summary of St. John's journey stages see Leonard Doohan, *The Contemporary Challenge of John of the Cross* (Washington, D.C.: ICS, 1995).

page 166   "not to gain ground is to lose": John of the Cross *The Ascent of Mount Carmel* 2.11.5, in *The Collected Works of Saint John of the Cross*, trans. Kieran Kavanaugh and Otilio Rodriguez (Washington, D.C.: ICS, 1991), p. 144.

page 166   John's fivefold journey paradigm: See Doohan, *Contemporary Challenge of John of the Cross*, p. 54.

page 167   five-stage journey paradigm: Evelyn Underhill, *Mysticism* (New York: Noonday, 1955), pp. 168-70.

page 167   M. Scott Peck outlines a four-stage journey paradigm: See M. Scott Peck, *The Different Drum* (New York: Simon & Schuster, 1987), chap. 9.

page 167   "manipulative and self-serving": Peck, *Different Drum*, p. 189.

page 168   one large community: Peck, *Different Drum*, p. 202.

page 168   "two steps ahead of us": Peck, *Different Drum*, p. 195.

pages 168-69 six-stage paradigm: Janet O. Hagberg and Robert A. Guelich, *The Critical Journey: Stages in the Life of Faith* (Salem, Wis.: Sheffield, 1995).

Names Index

Scripture Index